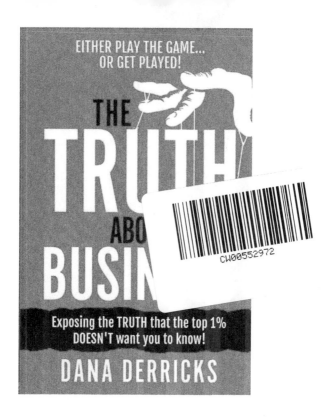

"Exposing The TRUTH That The 1% Doesn't Want You To Know..."

...Either Play The Game, Or Get Played!

Dana Derricks

"The Copywriting Professor"

Praise For Dana:

Most books have a few doctored up testimonials on the back cover, from buddies who were asked a favor to put their stamp of approval on it...without even reading it.

Some books have a handful of testimonials from folks that they bribed or paid for.

This one's different.

The praise I have, and why I humbly tell you to ditch everybody else and put your focus 100% into what I'm about to reveal to you, has been obtained with nothing less than more than a decade's working tirelessly in the trenches.

Like, actually doing it.

You can't fake this.

Go read the stories, here:

--> www.IsDanaLegit.com

^^ Yep, there's not nearly enough room to put all those in here. You'll see why this has been the best kept secret by page 37. Read on.

Disclaimer (Important):

Amendment I: Congress shall make no law prohibiting the free exercise thereof; or abridging the freedom of speech.

This book is going to ruffle feathers and upset many of business' top 1%, as this book exposes exactly how they play the game. It's time the world knows the truth. You'll see, soon.

Attorney's for the top 1%, please send your grievances to:
Billy the Goat
Counsel For The World-Famous Goat Farm
304 S. Jones Blvd #1031
Las Vegas NV, 89107

This book (and the concepts it distributes) contain business strategies, marketing methods and other business advice that, regardless of my own results and experience, may not produce the same results (or any results) for you. The TRUTH About Business makes absolutely no guarantee, expressed or implied, that by following the advice or content available will make any money or improve current profits, as there are several factors and variables that come into play regarding any given business.

Primarily, results will depend on the nature of the product or business model, the conditions of the marketplace, the experience of the individual, and situations and elements that are beyond your control. As with any business endeavor, you assume all risk related to investment and money based on your own discretion and at your own potential expense.

It's time to know the truth, and take back control.

Dedication

To the entrepreneurs out there looking to make an honest living...

Whom recognize that this journey isn't meant to be taken alone...

And whom are looking to put their dent in the world...

...this one's for you.

Special shout out to Russell Brunson, for championing many of the concepts in this book and supporting me to expand upon them to become this book. Buy all things Russell; you won't regret it.

Table of Contents

Dana Derricks

AKA "The Copywriting Professor"

& "Your Farmer Friend"

Email: support@dream100.zendesk.com

Website: www.DanaDerricks.com

Preface

always find myself wondering why people do the things they do. The gal cutting my hair, I ask, "What got you started in hairdressing?"

The Uber driver picking me up from the airport, "What did you do before?"

The guy cold-calling me asking if I want to list my rental property for sale, "Do you mostly do appointment setting for that realtor?"

Can't help it.

I like to know WHY.

Almost always, why we do what we do is far more important than what we do.

That's why I like to know.

I can tell a lot about a person and how my experience will be with them by simply getting that answer.

With that, I'll answer that for you.

The reason I've written this book is actually pretty simple.

I can't go another day watching how confused the people that think they have a business, but don't, are.

In fact, I would venture and go as far as saying that a LOT of people that think they have businesses, really don't have businesses.

Nope.

Instead, they just have products, or they have services.

That's it.

I'll prove it.

Ever see the TV show Shark Tank?

Nearly every episode, the latest amazing product or invention is balanced out by a complete, utter, painful-to-watch failure.

WAY too often, entrepreneurs will get absolutely blasted by the sharks (would-be investors) for this ONE reason...

They get tossed the reality check of, "Sorry, you're not a business, you're a product". Or, "Sorry, you're not a business, you're a service".

A nice, hard, slap right to the face.

...and it's just what they need, whether they know it at the time or not.

Although some of the sharks are harsher than others and can be very brutal, they're right.

A lot of these folks have great ideas for a product, or a service, or whatever. Even the ones that are further along and are already selling the product or the service, that still doesn't make it a business.

I know what you're thinking...

Okay, Dana, that's cool and I hear you.

But...what DOES make a business, a business?

Good thing you asked.

Even better, this book is your answer.

No MBA or business degree gives the answer.

Only a decade's worth of real, in-the-trenches work revealed it.

You get it, for FREE, inside the pages of this book.

Pretty cool, right?

Your task is to read this entire book.

Every. Page.

I hate to do this, but...

You're going to need to read it ALL, right now.

Yep, in ONE swoop.

So, tell your spouse you've got a project you'll need a few hours to finish.

Tell your kids daddy/mommy is busy for the next few hours planning their trip to Disneyworld.

Tell your pets that they could go a few days without food or water, so the few hours they're about to be ignored won't kill them.

Shut your phone off.

Delete your Facebook.

Okay, you don't have to full-blown delete it, but at least silence it.

Seems extreme?

Well, as you'll soon find out, my readers aren't like the rest of society.

They get lost in the pages of my books, because it's not a book.

It's an experience.

You'll find out, don't worry.

Anyway, I'll spill the biggest nugget of all, right now...

Ready?

...

...

..

.

..

...

...

Uh oh.

...

..

.

..

Printer

Running

Out

Of

Toner

...

..

.

..

...

..

.

..

...

.

..

...

Need

To

Conserve

Words

..

.

Just kidding. (Hope you're okay with a little fun, mixed in?)

Here it is.

The ONLY qualifier that dictates whether you have a real business, or you're just a product or a service is...

A fully built value ladder.

That's it.

If you want to have a real business, you need to have a value ladder, done right.

Even if you have no idea what a value ladder is and this is going to be completely new, you need to read this.

Even if you already know what a value ladder is but aren't quite sure how to build yours out the right way, you need to read this.

Even if you know what a value ladder is and have built one for yourself or clients, you need to read this.

Here's why.

Look at every single real business out there that does really, really well

I'm talking sustainable, real businesses that have been around for a while, not the one hit wonders.

Every single sustainable business that's been around for a long time (or will be around for a long time) has a fully built out value ladder.

Every. Single. One.

That's how important having a value ladder is.

It's not even optional in the competitive landscape we're currently in.

No longer can a person get away with running a decent business without one.

It's now a decision.

Either you have a business, or you don't.

It's literally that important.

Quick story that explains what it was like for me, years ago, with and without a value ladder, ceteris paribus.

^^ that's a fancy way to say, "all else equal". I need to sound as smart as possible in the first few pages of this book, before my true, goofy, down-to-earth personality comes bursting out like a caged animal...

Back in a previous lifetime, I was a freelance copywriter.

The kind that writes words that sells stuff, not the kind that writes words to patent things (copyrighter).

I had a copywriting service, and inherently thought I had a business because I was making a little bit of money.

Boy, was I wrong.

It was no business.

I was selling my copywriting services like most people sell their services.

Basically, the old, "Here's what I do, here's how much it is".

Pretty much everybody does that, right?

I can remember how difficult it was for me to land clients for a long, long time due to competing in extremely competitive markets.

It was very frustrating feeling trapped, knowing I was better than many others out there I was losing jobs to.

I was a commodity.

I mistakenly designed my business that way, not knowing what I didn't know.

I'll break it down for you...

People would come into my world cold and unfriendly.

They didn't know me from the next guy or gal.

I had to do a bunch of persuasion and work to figure out what the heck they needed. Then I had to prescribe a solution.

As the hours added up, I got better and better at it.

But, at the end of the day, I still wasn't a business.

Even as I commanded higher fees.

Even as projects started coming to me instead of me chasing them down.

I was just a service.

I could be easily compared to the next person, and a lot of times I did get compared to the next person.

That was always the worst part, because I knew I was more valuable than what I was getting paid for.

Can you relate to feeling undervalued or underestimated?

I felt it inside me.

I knew what I was worth, yet people wanted to compare me to the next person who wasn't as skilled as me, who wasn't going to produce the same quality service as me, and yet they STILL wanted to price me along with the other person.

I lost sleep because of it.

I knew there had to be a better way.

...and I found it.

When I started to understand and implement just a piece of the value ladder in my copywriting service, I started building an actual business.

Instead of having to put a smiling face on and answer a million questions, prospective clients came to me warm and red-hot...ready and excited to work with me.

Instead of feeling like I had to pry clients wallets open to get them to say yes to my proposals (I actually had a client one time say that's what it's like to get money from him, no joke)...clients came knocking on my door and throwing money at me to get me to work with them.

Instead of having to constantly reduce my fees or match the bids of my competitors, or risk losing the job...clients paid my fee without question, and I dictated the price!

Instead of being forced to be absolutely glued to my phone and feeling like my clients were worse than a boss at a J-O-B...I was able to work with only the BEST clients that I chose.

...and a whole lot more.

So, whether you've got a physical products business, a service, consultancy, coaching, information, software, local, global, you name it...

...a value ladder is your answer.

I know that there's a million different resources out there but, by the end of this book, I'll promise you this:

If you follow and implement all that I tell you to, you're going to 10x to 300x your business.

Yep, super bold.

But, thousands of folks can't be wrong, can they? (A little diligence doesn't hurt anybody --> www.IsDanaLegit.com)

There's not another strategy that can do this, with hardly any major changes.

Trust me, I've tried everything else.

So, if you're just getting started in this entrepreneurial journey and want to avoid the costly, time-stealing mistakes and do things right the first time, this book is for you.

If you've got questions around clarity on how to structure your offers and/or how to deliver them, this book is for you.

If you've got some clarity on what your offers are and how to deliver them, but want more, this book is for you.

If you're looking to build a rock solid, sustainable, real business that achieves what you've always known you have inside of you, this book is for you.

Let's get you clear withOUT overwhelm.

Shall we?

It's time to free you from the daily grind, and get you feeling like you have a solid plan to move forward with.

As long as you read through this entire book, right now, that's what'll happen.

You can sleep when you're dead. 😉

Introduction

I want you to know something. I'm an entrepreneur, just like you. I'm different, just like you. I have a big heart, just like you. I've been through a lot, just like you.

Unlike traditional books or resources, I've actually been there and done this.

I've put my 10,000 hours in.

I'm a fellow entrepreneur whose heard a million times, "you can't do that" or "that won't work".

I get it.

This book is probably one of the only books on Earth that you'll ever read, business books for sure, that you can literally stop and implement the strategies that I'm going to expose to you...and significantly impact your revenue immediately.

Literally, without making major changes, without dumping tons of resources, spending more time, energy and money, just follow my lead.

I won't make you learn a million different new things, either.

Just plug this into your existing thing and watch what happens.

That's the biggest takeaway you're about to get from this book.

Take just ONE strategy out of here, and you could see results by this time tomorrow, all right?

I know a lot of people write books for the wrong reasons.

Fame.

Money.

Ego.

I do not write books to get famous, rich, or pump my chest.

I'm a simple, friendly goat farmer from Wisconsin.

I don't need all the glitz and glamour.

I wear bib overalls.

I'm good.

This book exists because I think of my younger self, and I think of how I ran what I thought was a business for a long time.

How much I struggled.

The sleepless nights.

The not knowing if I'd be able to pay rent.

The NSF notices (if you've ever been poor, you know what the heck those are).

The abuse from clients.

The constant ups and downs and instability.

This book would have fixed everything, had it been around back then.

I want you to know that I'm here to help as many people as I can, and you're one of them.

I really mean it, and I want to put a dent in this planet.

Just so you know before you dive in, just remember, keep this in the back of your head.

Let this soak in.

Reading this book and implementing what's inside is going to give you full control and power to build a real and sustainable business.

With that being said, shut up Dana, let's dive in.

Chapter #1

"How A 5-Gallon Bucket, Hammer, & Life Insurance Forced Me To Make 7-Figures...FOUR Times!"

won't forget it. I'm sitting in my apartment office, which was already a huge upgrade for me. A dedicated room as my office that didn't have a bed, dresser, or TV competing for space, I finally "made it".

I've got some breathing room, for the first time.

$5,000 cash in my bank account.

That was more than I'd ever had, in my life.

Enough for 6 months' worth of living expenses.

I remember my mom always telling me to store up 6 months' worth of cash...but never expected it to feel this way.

It was liberating.

Empowering.

...and was the sole reason for my discovery of the Value Ladder...

The big discovery I had that day, and that I'll both share with you and dissect in this book, is pretty simple.

Before I get into it, I have to start with a dose of tough love...

In case you don't know, I used to coach football.

A lot of times, the method of coaching that worked best, and coincidentally the one that they needed the most, was a little "tough love".

I'll put my coaching hat back on for just a second...and lay it down like it is, okay?

I want you to stop what you're doing and drop to the floor.

Give me 10 pushups.

NOW.

One.

Two.

Three.

Four.

...oh wait.

Sorry, got carried away.

If you want to hit a set of 10, be my guest.

Okay, okay.

Here it is...

...sorry, but if you don't have a fully built value ladder, you are not a business.

Even if you've been featured on a cool magazine.

Even if you've made a million dollars.

Even if you have employees.

Even if you have customers or clients who would back you up.

You are either a product or you are a service.

By the end of this book, you'll agree with me wholeheartedly, trust me.

Quick back story on that.

In case you aren't quite familiar with what exactly a Value Ladder is, which is totally cool, let's zoom out and give you a 30,000-foot view...

A Value Ladder is the vehicle that allows you to sell more than one thing to the same person.

I remember I read a book years ago by a guy named Dan Kennedy, and he was explaining this concept that I was absolutely fascinated by.

He explained that, in his estimation, it was six times cheaper (and about 1,000 times easier) to sell the same exact object to somebody that has already bought from you than to try to sell it to a stranger, or someone that didn't previously buy from you.

I remember thinking to myself, "Holy crap, that makes a lot of sense."

Here I was, constantly thinking I needed to find new clients all the time.

For way too long, I ran my copywriting service like this (notice how I did NOT call it a business, because it wasn't)...

"Alright I've got this service, and that's what I do. That's my business, I just sell this service to people. The more people I can sell this to, the more money I'll make."

Reading that was a wakeup call because, prior to that, I hadn't even considered selling more to my existing clients (aside from the ones that came back asking for more).

I thought, "Holy crap, leveraging the concept of a Value Ladder means I can not only sell my service, but I can also sell additional things to people that are buying my service!"

I discovered more in that 10 minutes about business that I did in my entire 5 years to attain my Bachelor's Degree in Business Administration.

...and for about $41,985 less.

Forehead slap.

I didn't stop there.

I kept thinking about the possibilities and what this would open up for me.

Not only could I sell MORE to those whom DID buy my copywriting service...I could ALSO sell things to the people that did NOT.

Wait. A. Minute.

"You mean I can make money from EVERYBODY who comes into my world, not just the folks that say 'yes' to my proposal? ...what kind of sorcery is this?", I thought.

In ten minutes, I went from being a "me too", "yes or no" service...to being on the verge of being a REAL business...

...one that could sell to EVERYBODY that came in my world.

In my brain, I now knew that I could keep selling my existing service to new customers like I was...

PLUS I could sell something else to those that don't want (or couldn't afford) the service...

PLUS I could sell something else to the people that already bought the service...

Cha-ching.

It was a giant mind shift for me, which opened up all sorts of doors.

Imagine hitting one of those mushroom powerups in Super Mario World.

That was me.

Get outta the way, Dana's about to take over!

...and take over, I did.

Want me to map out my very simple Value Ladder that I personally used in my freelance copywriting business, to take it from a 5-figure..."me too" commodity...to an explosive, 7-figure, bullet proof business?

That'll be just one payment of $47.

Jk.

Two payments of $47...

Fine, fine.

I'll just show you.

This is what it looked like before I had the life-changing moment...

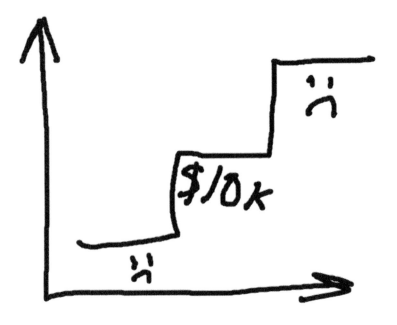

What I thought was my business, was actually just a service.

Here's what it looked like, after.

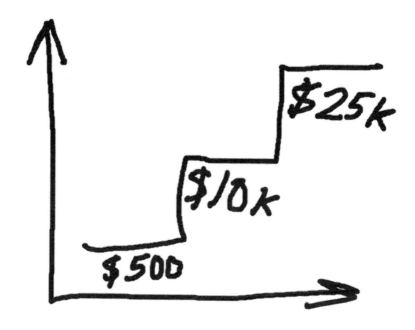

See the difference?

We're just scratching the surface...don't worry.

Ready for the best part?

This WILL work for you, because it literally works for every single kind of business.

Services.

Physical products.

Digital products.

Consulting.

Coaching.

Brick and mortar.

Freelance.

Agency.

Local.

Global.

Goat farms.

You name it.

It works.

I've not only seen this happening with every great company out there, but also have personally used it to do this...

I don't know if there are many people out there that have created at least a million-dollar service, a million-dollar physical products business, a million-dollar coaching and consulting business, and a million-dollar digital business.

I did.

100% on the leverage of a Value Ladder, every time.

Name a type of business you can launch, and I have made a million bucks in it because of the concept in this strategy of the Value Ladder.

As we continue to dive in and take this to the next level, an important way for you to think about this and anticipate how you'll implement it is to really focus on what you already sell.

What is it?

I don' t care what it is, it could be anything.

Pet products, haircuts, roofs, graphic design, renovation, vehicles, pens, services, insurance products, goats.

Whatever, it doesn't matter.

Think about what you already sell, and then think about what other products or services potentially could fit into your Value Ladder.

...and here's the golden rule of the Value Ladder.

This is REALLY cool, by the way.

You ready for it?

MAJOR nugget.

We're not even through chapter one, and you're getting one of the biggest nuggets you'll ever get.

Are you ready for this?

Crap...

Printer's making a strange noise...

I think that's a sign to tell me NOT to expose this one so soon in the book...

Meh, I'll take my chances. Just send me a nice Christmas Card 😊

NUGGET >> When you build out your Value Ladder, the number one thing you must do is to answer this question; how can I turn my customer back into a lead?

That's HUGE.

Took me a decade to figure that out.

You're much more fortunate, because you're tearing through this book.

I mentioned it before, but now really think about it...

When I had my freelance copywriting service, I was like, "Oh my gosh, I can sell something to people that already bought my service. Cool."

But then, it's like, "Okay, that's awesome, but WHAT do I sell them?"

I sat on that for a little while, then...BAM...it hit me!

It became crystal clear and glorious, like a brand spanking new pair of noise canceling headphones cranked to the max...while your spouse is asking you to do something and you just nod and smile...

By simply asking and answering the question of, "Dana, how can you turn your client back into a lead?"

I mapped it out...

Before they became my client, they were a lead, right?

They were either going to buy my thing or not.

The buyers became a client.

The non-buyers became broke, got divorced, and ended up in prison.

Only kidding. But their future was much less bright, I will admit.

Most people stop there, and they're like, "Oh cool, I got a new client, I'm done."

No.

No, no, no, no, no.

Imagine this for a second...

Where I grew up in rural Wisconsin, lots of more-crazy-than-me people find trees that produce sap, which they turn into maple syrup.

It's not as simple as it sounds...

You take 5-gallon bucket, a hammer, and a special "tapper" and head to the woods.

You trudge along in the cold (it's a fall thing), with your buckets and hammer, until you find a certain type of tree.

Once you find it, you pound the tapper into the side of it.

Whack! Whack! Whack!

The tree is cold, and it's bark solid, so you better swing hard.

You get the tapper in all the way, and hang the bucket by the handle...for the sap to drip in.

You repeat until you're too cold to move, you've got all the trees tapped, or you run out of buckets.

Whichever comes first.

Now, what's the lesson in this?

Simple.

What would be the DUMBEST thing a person could do, after putting in all that time/effort/energy?

Tap a tree for a little bit of sap, then move on to the next tree.

In other words, spending all that time and energy and effort to find the tree, to lug all your stuff up to the tree, to then pound your tapper into the tree and install the bucket, let it sit for a bit to gather sap, and then pull it off and leave and say, "Alright, I got some sap."

NO.

Go back to the tree and get more sap.

Let it drip ALL the sap before you rip the bucket away.

Same. Thing. With. Your. Customers.

They become a customer, congratulations.

WHY rip your bucket off so early?

Do a heck of a job over-delivering and LEAVE YOUR BUCKET there for them to buy more stuff.

Make sense?

Let's simplify and get practical.

Answer this: what do they need next?

How can you turn your customer or client back into a lead?

Think about pretty much any product out there, that you've seen on TV or anywhere else selling direct to consumer.

Think about these companies acquiring a customer, and then what would happen if they stopping and did NOT sell anything else to that customer.

Amazon assuming you're just going to buy once and be gone.

Netflix thinking you only want one movie.

How dumb is that?

That's what most businesses do, and what most entrepreneurs do.

It's crazy, but true.

Think about how much smarter it is to create an entire list of all those customers and then go back to them and sell them more stuff.

Remember Dan's insight of how much easier and cheaper it is to sell the same object to someone who's already bought from you...

...and how much you save on the resources to get their attention and build that trust.

I'll leave you with one more story, a local example of this in action.

I've got a buddy named Trent.

He sells insurance products in a town of, literally, 1,200 people.

(Not a typo)

Before you feel sorry for him or wonder why, Trent was the number two producer in the entire state last year in his company.

How the HECK did Trent do that?

You probably guessed it.

Trent's got this whole Value Ladder figured out.

I remember a few years back, sitting down with him.

I asked, "Trent, what's the absolute easiest, most brain-dead-simple thing for you to sell?"

He replied, "Auto insurance, everybody needs it. But, I hate selling it because there's pretty much no margin on it."

I said, "Great. Now what's the most lucrative thing that you sell, that puts the most money in YOUR pocket?"

He said, "Definitely life insurance. But, I have trouble selling that because every other agent is trying to sell it all the time."

"Perfect", I replied.

I gave Trent a quick lesson that took me years of struggling to find out, that quickly made me millions of dollars and will do the same for him (and, hopefully, you)...

I explained to Trent that he needed to STOP selling the 'thing' that everybody else was selling; life insurance.

Instead, I told him that he needs to sell the 'thing that sells the thing', and build out his Value Ladder.

In other words, I told him, "You're going to put your auto insurance offer as the beginning of your value ladder, and you're going to use that as your 'thing that sells the thing'.

So, you're going to sell the crap out of auto insurance NOT to make money, that doesn't matter. You're going to undercut people if you have to, and you're going to be known as the 'go-to insurance agent for auto', okay?"

Skeptical, but a lifelong friend, Trent nodded in agreement.

"If somebody needs auto insurance, talk to Trent. Go to Trent. Pretty soon, everybody's going to be moving over to you because you're the auto insurance guy, the guru."

Now, the whole point of that is so that Trent could use his Value Ladder, by getting customers in the door with auto insurance...using that as the thing that sells the thing.

After getting them in with auto insurance, he can then go back, after he's built that relationship with him...having gotten them to know/like/trust him AND open their wallet up.

Guess what he does, next?

He sells them life insurance.

He uses auto insurance as the thing that sells life insurance.

BAM.

See how he became the second-best producer in the entire state, which by this time next year I'm sure he'll be the number one, as he just opened up his own office and expanded expanded into a town of larger than 1,200...

All because he knows how to leverage a Value Ladder as his thing that sells the thing.

So, if you think this won't work for you, it works for everybody.

It's been the #1 reason for my ability to create a million dollar business in 4 different industries...

It's working for literally thousands of my clients...

It's working for Trent in a tiny little town in Wisconsin

Yes, it's going to work for you...but only if you keep reading.

Next up, I'll explain a little deeper on what the biggest, most excruciating mistakes are with building out your Value Ladder...that leave some well-intended entrepreneurs on a fast-path to failure...

You can't miss that, can you?

Chapter 2

"Why Going To The Bathroom Cost Me $1,000...And How 'Process Of Eliminationing It' Is The Best Way To Murder Your Business..."

Having wasted around $250,000 on crummy programs, courses, coaches, agencies, and more over the years...I can with 1,000% confidence say that investing your time/money/energy/attention into this Value Ladder concept is pretty much every other option you could possibly do for your business.

I mean, it's the thing that actually unlocks your business as a real business.

I also would know because I've done like every other thing.

Getting your Value Ladder right is the only way to truly explode your revenue without making major changes, spending tons of money, or crazy learning curves.

If you're like me, you've probably tried different things to expand your revenue, haven't you?

EVERYBODY claims to help drive more revenue.

One of the many things that I've tried and has left the worst taste in my mouth, is hiring folks like marketing agencies that promise the moon, but they deliver nothing.

The taste is so bad and so vivid, it's very much like the one-and-only time I picked up a Cherry Coke bottle in my dad's pickup truck.

It was August.

Around 85 degrees, very humid.

I had full jeans and a long sleeve tshirt on, not because it was practical.

Because I had been loading up haybales all afternoon and didn't want to get scraped up.

I was drenched in sweat and had managed to finish loading up the last wagon of the day.

I hopped into my dad's farm truck, which had no air conditioning.

Only a window that rolled down by hand.

Hot, sweaty, and ready to get out of my dirty clothes and take refuge in the shower...I made my first of two critical mistakes.

I had forgotten my water bottle on the hay wagon.

Already on my way back home, there was NO way I was about to pull over to go grab it.

Mistake #1.

Instead, I glanced over at the cup holder in the center console of the truck.

In it sat two drinks, an empty Diet Mountain Dew bottle, which has always been my dad's drink of choice...and about a third full Cherry Coke.

I decided to take a couple swigs of the Cherry Coke, to get the dust and dryness out of my mouth.

Mistake #2.

As a vulnerable human being that was overly thirsty and trusting, I didn't bother to sniff it or take a sip.

Nope.

I gulped.

The first gulp alarmed me that something was terribly wrong.

Unfortunately, my instincts and involuntary response didn't kick-in in time to spare me from taking a second...

Upon the second gulp, it all came right back up.

All over the dashboard and steering wheel.

I was in shock and it was all I could do to keep the truck and load of hay on the road.

 What. Just. Happened. To. Me.

I wondered...

...and then it hit me.

I had just been the victim of a MAJORLY "frowned-upon" and unwritten rule of farmers.

My brother had left his chewing tobacco-spitter in the truck.

Perfectly disguised as an innocent, refreshing Cherry Coke.

I learned my lesson, that day.

I still, to this day, opt for cans of soda and give any bottle the "sniff test" to make sure.

It was that traumatic.

...here's why I tell you that story.

To let you know that, as bad as that physically left a terrible taste in my mouth that's forever changed me...

What I've gone through with these 'marketing agencies' is WORSE.

Yep, I'd rather chug an ENTIRE bottle of that "homemade Cherry Coke" than to even THINK about giving another dime of my money to them.

More on that, in a second.

That's one route that I've gone and have tried a ton in the past.

Add to that the decade to literally learn it all myself, and then try 7,000 different things along the way to finally sift through and find the handful of gems...which is extremely expensive and exhausting, by the way.

That's not the worst thing a person could do, though...

The absolute WORST thing that anybody could do is to try and just keep doing what they're doing with expecting a different result.

It's like Albert Einstein says.

The definition of insanity.

Here's the good news, for you...

One thing I've never done is sit and wait for things to happen.

I've always tried, tried, tried, and tried.

That got me into trouble a lot, but it also definitely got me where I am.

What's awesome is that YOU are about to leverage the heck out of my lessons from wasting a quarter million dollars, my 'never-giving-up', and my trying and failing on 6,995 of the 7,000 different things I tried over the years.

Sound good?

I could go on and on about why those alternative paths are terrible…which I may in a later chapter if I feel a good rant coming…but I'll just briefly say this.

First, marketing agencies, if you just think about it common-sensically about it, they shouldn't really exist.

Why?

Because if they were so good at marketing, they would simply just market their own offers.

Think about it this way.

Would you hire an out-of-shape personal trainer, or let your children ride on a bus with the bus driver with no driver's license? No.

That's what marketing agencies are.

They're the overweight personal trainer that doesn't follow their own advice, or they're the bus driver that doesn't even have a driver's license because they never drive, or that shows people how to drive buses, and never drives a bus.

Hiring agencies to take care of this stuff almost always ends bad. I've wasted enough to make darn sure.

Then, the whole "taking a decade to learn it on your own" (like I die) is a terrible idea because I would realistically estimate that 95%, and I say this with the utmost amount of confidence, of what people sell online is absolute garbage and shiny objects.

Let that sink in a bit, I'll prove it by the end of this book.

The last thing that I know you're not doing (because you're reading this), but others do wrong, is sitting around for something to happen.

As you know, nothing will magically change.

It'll take some trial and effort.

But, it's incredibly worth it.

Real quick story...

A lot less wise version of myself decided to entrust in a marketing agency.

They seemed awesome.

Super nice gal, running it.

I hate to admit it, but I've actually hired several since this...with similar results...but this one takes the cake.

I call it, excuse me here, but my $1,000 dump story.

So I hired this Facebook Ads agency.

I, obviously, get promised the moon, like they do.

I send them money. Lots of money.

They go in, make a bunch of changes and appear to have been extremely busy.

I remember them checking in, telling me, "Yeah, all you need to do is just look at the campaign, make sure it looks good. Then when it does, just press go on this button."

I'm like, "Okay, sounds good?"

Looking back, I think that was their way of, you know how like if somebody else presses the button to ignite the nuclear bomb, technically, you didn't do it.

It was, basically, that.

They made me pull the trigger so that then, technically, they weren't responsible.

I guess red flag number 60, before hiring this agency, was them making me pull the trigger.

Man, I just didn't know the gun was pointed at my head.

Anyway, I digress.

I pressed the trigger, and I didn't even know what they were doing. I knew nothing about it.

They said it was completely hands-off, which I was excited about, frankly, because I didn't want to have to learn all that crap. I pressed go on it, and sorry to give you this visual, but I had to go to the bathroom.

I went to the bathroom and was in there maybe 10 minutes, whatever.

My bathroom is not far away, by the way. It's just a few steps.

I go in there, go to the bathroom, and come back out. I check on it, and I kid you not, I crap you not, no pun intended, pun intended, I had blown through $1,000.

Yep, $1,000 was gone, extracted from me.

While in the bathroom.

Seems a bit outrageous, to be robbed that quickly?

I had no idea how or why, or where that money went.

To this day, I don't know where it went.

The worst part of it all is that I had nothing to show for it. I didn't have any more leads. I didn't have any more customers. I had nothing. I didn't even know where it went.

I remember that keeping me up that night...thinking, "Shoot, Dana. If you were to go to a casino and throw $1,000, at least you can see where the hole that the money goes."

Like I'm sure you, I can think of a lot better things to waste $1,000 on.

Any who, we don't really make mistakes...as long as we draw a lesson from it.

Hopefully you don't relate to that story but, if you do, just know you're definitely not alone...

I'm sure you can relate to this, though.

One of the most accurate adjectives I'd like anybody to know me as...is stubborn.

Not the argue politics kind of stubborn...but the relentlessly chasing your dreams kind.

As a fellow entrepreneur, you know you need a level of this in order to survive in our world.

BUT...it also can be a detriment if you don't know when to stop. Not when to give up, but to stop, and then tweak, and continue.

Know what I mean?

In my mind, I'm going through trying different things until I find something that works.

When I was starting, I felt overwhelmed with all these different opportunities and directions.

It was like being whisked into an entirely new world.

Ever feel that way?

I was pulled in a bunch of directions; many were fun and felt like an adventure.

I was excited.

I would try different things, one after the other.

One time, I staying up all night reading this guide on how to invest in real estate with no money down. I remember being so excited about that, and it literally kept me up all night.

What a fantastic opportunity, it seemed.

I quickly got in the habit of buying stuff and trying it.

New opportunities, all the time.

Then, it always came back to pretty much the same thing over and over.

One common theme emerged...I'd buy into the whole idea of the opportunity and what I was being pitched, but it really wasn't right for me.

I came to realize that these were either not the right opportunities for me, or the timing wasn't right.

It wasn't paying the bills.

This is the problem I ran into and what I did wrong.

For many years, I was trying what felt like a billion different things.

Ever felt that way?

We're conditioned through school to use this thing called the process of elimination to solve problems, right?

We take an exam, and it makes sense to use it.

During the exam, we're given multiple choices of possible answers.

It could be A, B, C or D.

We read the question.

Then, we think about what the answer could be.

Then, we look at the answers they give us, A, B, C or D.

A, we know it's wrong.

We cross it off.

B, same thing.

C, same thing.

D, same thing.

A lot of times, you're able to eliminate most, if not all, of the incorrect answers...leaving you with a very high likelihood of getting the correct one.

I'm thinking to myself, "Shoot, that must apply to the real world."

I mistakenly thought that, like an exam, there were only so many things I could try before I found one that actually worked.

I "process of elimination'd" it for a long time.

Pretty soon, I blew through the whole Alphabet.

I not only eliminated A through C.

Shoot, I eliminated A through Z.

The crummy part is that, in the real world, the amount of inputs, unlike an exam, is not finite.

It means that there are WAY more potential outcomes in the real world than on an exam question.

The sheer number of opportunities we can chase to make money is more than we could even get through in a lifetime.

In other words, for every opportunity that I'd tried and that didn't work, I'd cross it off.

While I was busy trying that one opportunity and crossing it off after finding out it didn't work as promised, 10 more were created.

I realized, not quickly enough, that this process of elimination, this try, try, try until I find something that works, really wasn't a winning strategy.

If you're like me, and you're just too dang stubborn to quit, you're my people.

You're going to really, really enjoy what the Value Ladder done right does for you.

Lastly, the direction some take is to sit around wait for things to happen for them.

I can remember seeing this in high school and, even, predicting it. I had a buddy that I played football with.

Cool kid, and all that.

He was really laid back and just let things come to him. I have absolutely no fear of him reading this book, by the way, because it'll prove my point.

Anyway, I remember in high school we were all planning to do our ACT exam and apply for colleges. He was very laid back about it.

I can remember him repeating to us, "Yeah, I'll do that next week probably, or whatever," and just sat around waiting for stuff to happen for him.

I felt so bad for him because we all left for college, and he didn't. He went to work at a factory.

More than smart enough to go to school or launch a business. He played it safe and waited.

We'd return home for holidays and hear him tell us, "Yeah, I'll go to school next year."

His famous phrase was, "Yeah, I'm going to do it, I will do it. Yeah, I'll do it."

As you can imagine, he never did it.

More than a decade later, and he still works at the same exact job at the same exact factory.

It's all because he waited around for other people to make the first move, for something to magically happen, or the "timing to be right".

It'll never come.

The people that wait, wait, wait, are the ones that die with regrets.

Remember how I mentioned at the top of the book I really like to know WHY people do things?

Well, here's another quick example...

WHY do the marketing "gurus" or agencies do what they do?

Well, we live in a world where "fluff" and "got ya" is nearly accepted.

What you buy is almost always never what you actually get.

Think of this.

Ever seen a Hardee's commercial?

They advertise those thick burgers, which, by the way, are delicious. I have absolutely indulged in those from time to time, I will shamefully admit it.

When they advertise them, first of all, they're absolutely perfect looking.

Flawless, in the commercial.

Far from what you're going to get when you go into the drive through.

If that's not enough, who do they have chomping them down?

Supermodels.

Supermodels that would never eat them, anyway.

Reminds me.

I actually had a client one-time, years ago, that did product photo shoots for a major brand.

He revealed everything to me, by the way.

In order to get that burger that perfect, you know what they would do?

This kind of thing...

He told me this example with cereal, one of his many foods he would photograph.

He said they were doing a product shoot for a brand of cereal. They brought in 10 giant bags of it.

They had two interns with tweezers dump the bags on the counter and pick through, one by one, to get only the perfect pieces.

For. Three. Straight. Hours.

They would fill the bowl with only the perfect ones.

To get exactly what they sell us on the commercial, we'd have to buy 10 giant bags, and spend more than three hours sifting through.

Here's an even crazier one...

Have you ever seen a commercial for pancakes or waffles, like maybe iHop or Waffle House?

When you see that stack of pancakes or waffles, it looks outrageously fluffy and perfect, right?

Then, you see that perfectly golden syrup being poured on it, and it runs down the side just perfectly.

I haven't eaten pancakes in a while, but what I remember about syrup pouring on them is this...the minute you pour, it gets absorbed right into it.

I'd have to dump a lot of syrup for it to actually drizzle over perfectly like it does.

Guess why the commercial looks so much better.

It's not syrup they pour on the pancakes.

Got a guess what it is?

Motor oil.

It's not even syrup.

Not even something that's edible.

Can you believe that? How's that even legal? Why is that legal?

That's just the world we live in.

It's fluff.

Most stuff isn't real.

That's why it takes people like me 10 years to get where we are, because I have to find out the hard way.

Eating enough motor oil, I suppose, will teach a person.

Here's the cold, hard truth.

Ready?

The reality is this.

The few who do know that this stuff works and that are using it, they're just behind the scenes using it and making lots of money and scaling their businesses like crazy.

These marketing agencies, if their stuff worked, they'd just be behind the scenes making money using it.

I know this because many of the silent, REAL experts are friends of mine.

Common sense hat back on for a second.

I went on this search for the best Facebook Ads person.

All I wanted was to find and work with the best Facebook Ads person.

I was even referred to the best ones, that I thought, and they ran these agencies.

I'm like, "Okay, great. You're probably an expert."

They suck.

One after the other.

They all suck, every single one of them. I've spent enough money to earn the right to say that.

With that being said, you want to know where the best Facebook Ads people are hiding?

They aren't selling that as a service.

They're. Running. Their. Company.

RAKING in the rewards of their real, authentic expertise.

They've blown up their company because of it.

Let's look at a quick example.

I met two very good friends when they were pretty much broke, or extremely broke, respectively.

Brandon Poulin, co-founder of LadyBoss.

Zero to $40 million in under 3 years.

Also, ironically, one of the best Facebook Ads people on earth.

He's also not for hire.

Then we have Alex Hormozi. Co-founder of Gym Launch.

Zero to $50 million in under 3 years.

Also one of the best Facebook Ads people on earth.

He's not for hire, either.

Ironic?

Coincidence?

Nah.

The reason that the Value Ladder thing is so awesome, by the way, is because it doesn't require you to find these geniuses.

You don't need a "guru" for this or that.

Just follow my lead.

Even better?

It also doesn't require you to chase a new, shiny object all the time.

Just a few simple tweaks to what you're ALREADY doing, simply follow what's in this book.

A few simple tweaks later, and bam!

I'll prove it.

Check this out.

Want to literally, by tomorrow, add 20% to 40% more revenue? Maybe even more.

Ready?

Let's do it.

Back when I was doing my freelance copywriting, I was working with clients doing projects and all that good stuff.

At the time, I was still either yes or no, you want to buy my service?

Not a business.

Here's what happened.

The majority of people said, "No" to my proposal because they couldn't afford it...OR they didn't have enough trust built up with me.

Guess what I did with those people.

The same thing almost everybody does.

I said, "Okay, talk to you later."

I'd send them down the road packing.

Usually, they'd end up at my competitor...whom warmly welcomed them and patted them on the back explaining how they had "made the right choice".

I still cringe from that.

Why'd I do that for so long?

I had no idea what to do with them.

I didn't even think there was a possibility to do anything with them.

After all, they didn't want to work with me?

Wrong.

Check this out.

I literally was able to monetize the people that said "no" to my service by building just ONE little piece of my Value Ladder.

By simply adding one more little piece I was able now have an answer for their "no"...

...and that became my down sell.

In other words, if they couldn't afford my proposal, or they're not ready to invest for whatever reason, the sale was NO long lost...like it had been before.

Instead of, "Okay I wish you the best" and sending them off to the knock-offs...I'd say, "Tell you what. I could take out this piece, and I could remove that. I could tweak my proposal so that we can bring it down to this price. What do you think?"

BAM!

Nearly everybody took my down sell.

To my surprise, the folks that were giving me a "no" weren't NOT interested in working with me...like I had though...but were not interested in the offer I was presenting.

Switch up the offer and the price, and we're back in business!

Literally, overnight, my service became a business.

I never thought it would work.

I honestly thought that when someone said, "no", their mind was made up and it was over.

Couldn't have been less true.

They want something.

They came to me for a reason.

It was MY job to give them the answer to their problem, in a way that worked for them.

Just because the thing you offer them isn't exactly what they want right then and there, doesn't mean something else similar to it won't be.

When you put a pencil to your time and fulfillment cost on your core offer versus your downsell...you might eventually make MORE money from your downsell!

This is what happened to me.

Check this out...

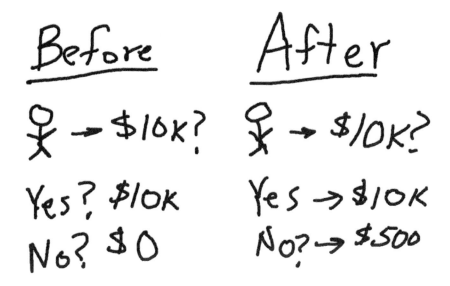

Before	After
☿ → $10k?	☿ → $10k?
Yes? $10k	Yes → $10k
No? $0	No? → $500

See how much of a hole I plugged by adding that downsell, and how much money I was leaving on the table?

Although the down sell wasn't as valuable of a transaction as my core offer, it increased my revenue by 40% overnight.

Yep, this stuff's real.

See how easy that is?

I want you to do that for tomorrow.

Think about where your leads that say, "No" to your main thing where they bounce, where they fall off, figure out what you can downsell to.

Crap.

If you think that's pretty sweet, we're only in chapter 2.

By the end of this book, your Value Ladder is going to be FULLY built, and you're going to be absolutely cranking.

Watch what I reveal in the next chapter...

(it may shock you, so please read NOW just in case)

Chapter #3

"How Scared Dogs And A Guy With A Thick Mustache PREVENTED Me From Being In The 90% Of FAILURES..."

T he moment I made the discovery of this whole Discover the Value Ladder concept, I was overcome by something fairly unexpected...

I felt suddenly humbled.

One of those, "Wow, I really have a lot more to learn" kind of moments.

Know what I mean?

It forced me back into the reality of understanding that just because I thought something didn't mean it was necessarily true...or make it correct.

I If you're like me, you're different, you think differently than most of the rest of society as an entrepreneur. Right?

One of the things that I get sucked into from time to time is playing the comparison game.

Comparing myself to the next guy. The next business. The next guru.

Even back before I was doing as well as I am now, I'd look at folks around me and think, "Wow, I make money from home or while I'm sleeping...or I have so much freedom that these people don't have. I make way more money than them, and I work way less than they do, and I get to call the shots."

I took a look in the mirror, and realized that me viewing those folks that way is no different than somebody who is better positioned than I am doing that to me and thinking that stuff about me.

I obviously never said those thoughts out loud or to anyone, but I said them to myself.

What I realized, quickly, was the reason I was having those thoughts was because I wasn't happy with where I was.

Straight up.

I told myself those things to make myself feel better and justify where I was.

^^ That right there is super dangerous.

It's literally the formula for complacency, AKA the "Anti-Growth Method".

You already know as a business owner, if you aren't growing...you're dying. It's a choice.

With that being said, tying it back into the POWER of the Value Ladder...I remember the first time I started implementing and how excited I was.

It was one of those ultra-rare occasions where I tried something that actually worked.

Know the feeling?

As excited and empowered as I was...I had another, less enjoyable feeling that kept creeping up, stronger and stronger...

Here's what happened.

As I'm mapping out my Value Ladder and literally transforming my business right on my desk...it hit me.

That all looks good on paper, BUT...the amount of work there was left to do stared me right in the face.

Another glaring reminder of how far I was from where I wanted to be.

It all stemmed from having the idea in my head that I was running a business. I wasn't, I was a service.

That's it.

So, like what I experienced, I'm giving you permission to be humble, reset and recalibrate, and grow.

Let's get back to it.

It doesn't matter where you are.

In fact, I know a lot more about you than you may think...

Sure, I can't see you or hear you as you plow through the pages of this book...but...

...it's scary how much I know about you, because I am you.

I've walked your walk.

I know, on one hand, you're the type of person that knows things will never be quite good enough, no matter what, and you have a fire inside of you that you obtained somewhere along the way in your life...that you'll NEVER allow to die no matter what happens. You'd rather die than let that fire out.

Right?

BUT...also, I know that you have to be realistic and smart because we live in a world where you need to make money, you need to have a level of sustainability and comfort in your life in order to survive and provide, and blindly following your passions, alone, isn't going to cut it.

Also right?

There's a balance.

Both of these thoughts have to work in tandem with each other. You put those two together and that's what growth is, and I've never seen a strategy ever before that encompasses both so beautifully as this concept of the Value Ladder.

So, whether you already understand what a Value Ladder is, you have one at least partially built up, or think this, "I know, Dana, I need a Value Ladder, I get it."

Your mind is about to be absolutely blown, soon, because I have taken the Value Ladder to the three billionth degree and...just wait. It's going to be fun.

The pages of this book are going to begin turning into gold, very soon...your job is to keep reading.

To start, we need to actually REdefine what a business actually is.

The measuring stick for what a business is that most people use, frankly, is dead wrong.

I see all the time people saying, "Oh, I'm a business owner," I'm this. I'm that.

And at the end of the day, the measuring stick historically has always been well, how much revenue are you generating?

Right?

Even worse, the thing that separates the "wantrepreneurs" from the entrepreneurs, isn't easy to spot withOUT what I'm about to share with you.

Folks think that just because the minute you make $100,000, or a million dollars, or whatever, all of the sudden you're a "business".

Wrong.

I see people that make that kind of money but then they have ZERO net profit.

I think to myself when I see them brag about it or post their out-of-context screen shots, "Congratulations, you made a million dollars last year, but you spent $950,000 in advertising, labor, and everything else to make the million".

That's like having a big fancy house, but inside it's completely bare. There's not even a couch or a bed, or anything in the kitchen.

Like, wow, that must be miserable to walk around an empty house that doesn't even have power.

Right?

What if these "successful business owners" shared what's REALLY going on?

It's easy to prove they're full of it.

Almost all of them.

Cool screenshot of gross income.

Now, how about we see like...ya know...something real?

Maybe a balance sheet?

*Gasps.

Income statement?

*Crickets.

I digress.

Let's build a REAL business, shall we?

A business that not only does generate lots of gross revenue, obviously, but it's got a fully built out Value Ladder so there's PROFIT.

Cool?

In the world we live in and how competitive it's gotten, there's just no way to have a great business without having a fully built out Value Ladder.

Either adopt it, or get left behind.

Having this "aha moment" for me with the Value Ladder probably contributed to the biggest takeoff in my entire career, in terms of the what I call explosive growth of my company.

It looked sort of like this...

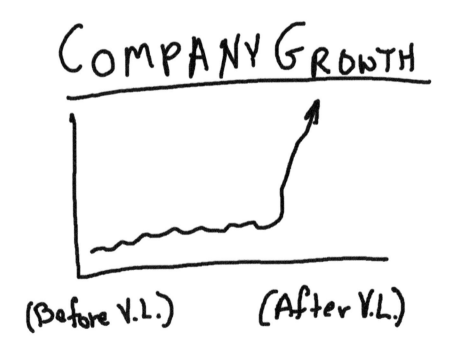

COMPANY GROWTH

(Before V.L.)   (After V.L.)

I've always done fairly well at improving, and up until then I had always slowly grown.

But when I doubled-down and started leveraging the Value Ladder, not only did it affect my business, but it also affected EVERYBODY around me.

My students.

My clients.

My friends.

Everybody got the goods.

I told you about my friend, Trent, in a tiny little Wisconsin town.

How his life has been forever changed because of this.

It's real.

Use it.

One of the coolest things I think that happened was after I had humbled myself to know that I needed to build a real business, and not just be a single offer, my mind shifted to...

"Holy crap Dana, the other stuff I've been doing and offering, that's just to get people in the door. ALL of the money is made in the back-end!"

For me, this was the moment.

It was like I had just struck oil.

I realized that what I THOUGHT made folks give me money and that my business needed (and that I sold) wasn't...

I figured out that, in actuality, the front end is the thing that everybody sees.

It's like the sign when you drive past a restaurant that says, "$1 Burgers Tonight 7-10pm"

They saw that BEFORE they even got their hands on the menu, which is the thing that actually sells their product.

See how that works?

Your front end is what everybody sees, but is NOT how a business should make the majority of it's money.

The front end is how they get us in the door.

Once we're in the door, the money is made by them upselling us other products or services.

We sit down to grab our $1 burger.

The waitress asks if you want to start with an appetizer, wings sound pretty good.

Then, she asks what we're drinking.

We're thirsty.

Then, when she takes our order, she asks if we want to upgrade to a double for only $3 more.

Dang.

Got us again.

THAT is where the money's made, in the back-end.

The appetizer.

The drinks.

The upgrade.

Sure, there are plenty of companies out there that make money on just front end.

That's really BAD because they're sitting on gold, and they don't scoop it up.

I could list countless examples, but I'm sure you now understand the difference between the two.

Quick lesson...

I get people that ask me all the time, "Dana how in the world? You sell books for thousands of dollars per copy, that doesn't make sense."

I agree, it doesn't make logical sense.

The secret is this...

It all started when I was working as a freelance writer.

I honed-in and served the Amazon seller niche for a long time.

Eventually, I started getting burnt out because, although I was doing extremely welll with making money, I was working WAY too much.

I piled the projects on and was drowning in work and money, which is a great problem, don't get me wrong.

The point is that I had to get out.

No more trading time for dollars.

Instead, I bundled up what I was selling in my service and put it into a concise, to-the-point book.

In other words, instead of being hired to catch the fish...I put together a book that would show folks how to catch their own.

Make sense?

THAT tweak, alone, was responsible for an incredible amount of impact, helped me instantly make a name for myself, and generated millions of dollars for me in this niche.

All because of the Value Ladder.

Here's how it worked, for me...

I sold almost 150 copies (with no ad spend by the way) to just under 70 countries $397 per copy.

The book?

Not even hard cover.

Good margins.

How?

I used it as BOTH a front-end offer...you'd be shocked at how many people would read that book and then want me to take care of their listings for them AFTER reading it...

...AND I used it as a down sell for my Amazon Listing Optimization service.

If somebody didn't have the budget or wasn't quite ready to pull the trigger on my $10,000/listing service...I'd simply sell them my book for $397 and dang near everybody took the offer.

Boom.

I didn't stop there...

I thought, "Dang...selling a book for hundreds of dollars is pretty cool, because the margins are fantastic, and the fulfillment is easy".

So, I wrote a sequel.

The sequel simply solved the next problem.

For context, the next book was a bit thicker and longer, and helped Amazon sellers to maximize their email follow ups.

You see, when you buy something on Amazon, the smart sellers, the ones that do really well, send you emails afterwards, delivering more value.

It hit me, "Holy crap, this isn't just an Amazon email book that shows them how to absolutely optimize email follow up campaigns, but it actually is a book that helps them to tap into the secret back-end where all the money is made".

DING! DING! DING!

No different than what I just exposed to you, about how the majority of money is made on the back-end...that started rippling to my students and customers.

Fast-forward and I launched another book, which sold for $1,500 per copy.

Yep, a book, still not hard cover, sold for $1,500 per copy.

I've sold over 130 copies, to date.

Still, zero ad spend.

Value Ladder > every other strategy

I didn't stop there, of course.

Doing this whole "Make my clients really rich" thing got old, after a while.

I started selling on Amazon, myself.

Within 6 months, I launched my own seven-figure eCom business in selling pet supplements.

Guess what strategy I leveraged?

Value Ladder.

I would have a bunch of singular, one-off products for sale, that were priced very competitively.

I didn't need to make money on them, they were my front-end.

Get them in the door.

I would get people in the door with those, but then guess what I did?

I cash-in on the back-end with my email follow ups.

I made a ton of money from that.

I'll literally break it down for you, cool?

Let's look back at the Value Ladder.

Here's my front-end.

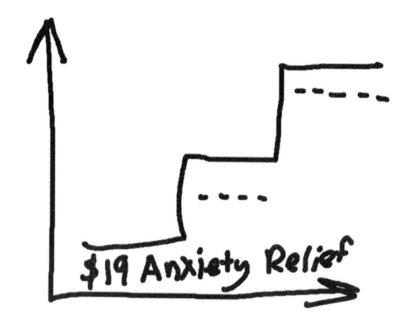

$19 Anxiety Relief

When it comes to the back-end, especially with physical products, I found out that there are, essentially, two different things you can offer...which I'll get into that more in detail in a bit here...

One of them (being the easiest thing to offer next) is NOT the default for people when they brainstorm what they should follow-up with or upsell.

It's so freaking simple, too.

Those that do it terribly wrong think, "Okay, they bought that thing, now what else can we sell them?"

No, it's like, "Okay, they bought that thing, sell them more of that thing."

I call it a more of the same offer, or "MOS".

Sell them more of the same exact thing they just bought.

Almost every time that will convert higher than plugging in any other offer.

Don't believe me? Test it.

I couldn't beat it over the past decade of testing. It works.

Here's what it looked like in my pet supplements business:

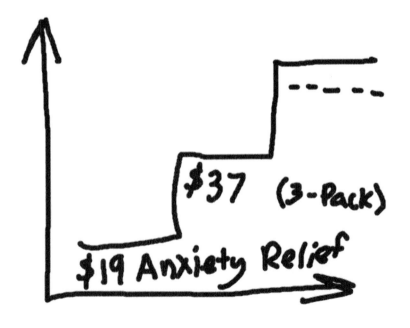

People will want that more than anything else you can offer them, almost always.

I'll prove it.

Think about everything you buy.

You go to a shoe store, you buy some shoes, or a boot store, for me. I buy some boots.

Should they sell me a saddle next?

Or, should they sell a gym bag or a duffle bag next?

No.

I came for boots.

They should sell me more boots.

It just makes sense.

That's the first option to build out a physical products Value Ladder, and I'll deep dive on this in a bit.

Crap, it's not just physical products.

It works with everything, literally.

When you buy tickets to a concert or sports event, should they sell you...water bottles?

No.

They should sell you MORE FREAKING TICKETS.

"Would you like to add another ticket to your order for only $69?"

When you reserve a hotel room, should they sell you...a restaurant voucher?

No.

They should sell you MORE FREAKING HOTEL ROOMS.

"Would you like to extend your stay by 1 night for only $99?"

That's MOS.

It's like that old, rusty-but-trusty truck.

Not glamorous.

Not sophisticated.

Not even exciting.

It. Just. Works.

Put it to work.

Then, we have the other option that I found that will work.

I found this one out back in college.

Years ago, I had a motorcycle.

(PSA: Don't let your kid ever buy a motorcycle under any circumstance lol)

It wasn't a regular motorcycle.

I had what they call a "crotch rocket".

Yep.

Shake your head.

I don't blame you.

The only justification I can give you, besides because I thought I was cool, was because of parking.

You can park almost anywhere for basically free and which was absolutely amazing living in a city.

I remember going to this gas station with it after class...and one of the most funny/awkward moments happened.

I go to this gas station, and I fill it up the gas tank.

I chose the pay inside option or whatever, and the attendant usually comes on to say, "Okay, you're good on pump 10. We'll see you inside."

Not this attendant.

This one was a trained assassin.

A stone-cold hustler.

She tried to upsell me.

She said over the loudspeaker, "Hey, you're good to go on pump 10. Would you like a car wash today?"

Typically, they look at you, and if you nod yes they'll throw it on your order and you get your code on the receipt to redeem it.

...the second after she uttered the words, I stood there, started...

I'm like, "What are you talking about?"

I'm standing next to my motorcycle, confused.

For a split-second, I actually second-guessed myself, "Wait...have I been washing my motorcycle wrong this whole time? Am I supposed to ride it through the car wash?"

haha

"Oh crap, sorry", I hear...snapping me out of my confusion.

^^ that's why it's so important to get your next offer RIGHT.

It can be disastrous and awkward, if you don't.

This starting to all make sense?

Awesome.

We're just scratching the surface.

Let's keep rolling.

The point of my motorcycle carwash story is that there are going to be times when a more of the same offer doesn't make sense, or the next thing doesn't make sense, which is why it's critical to be clear of your client or customer journey.

We've gone through the "MOS" offer, now let's explore the other type of offer...to blow up your business like a fuel truck slamming head-on into a fireworks store.

Big boom.

The other type of offer to upsell your first offer (or the next "rung" on your value ladder) is a "CO" offer, or a complementary offer.

For example, let's go back to the mall.

I buy a pair of boots.

This time, instead of offering me more boots (MOS), they offer the oil to protect them (CO).

This CO works so well because it's a no-brainer.

The best CO's I've seen that convert like crazy are ones that enhance the original offer.

"Enhance" means they make it:

> Last longer

> Work better

> Work faster

> Work more reliably

> Negate negative side effects

> Give a better overall experience

Here's how critical it is to not just use and leverage a Value Ladder...but also absolutely NAIL the type of offer you're going to deploy...

Not just that, but also DOING it.

Too many "coaches" or "gurus" talk about something, but never actually help you to deploy it.

Right?

So, let's actually deploy this and show you WHAT that looks like, shall we?

Deploying your Value Ladder isn't hard, don't worry.

The biggest thing is to STOP thinking as if selling is a singular transaction.

Remember the guided experience from before?

That's what we need to do.

In order to do that, we stop thinking singular, and start thinking about our business and how the marketing and sales fit together.

The best way to explain it is to look at is as if you're "funneling" your traffic, your buyers, and everybody that enters your world into and through your Value Ladder.

As they come into your world, you "funnel" everybody into the front end of your Value Ladder, and naturally some will continue to ascend through it.

No different than when ranchers funnel their cattle into a large pen, then pluck the ones they want to separate into smaller shoots.

Best part?

You can do this online.

24/7.

Anywhere in the world.

Instead of having a traditional website or ecommerce store, building a funnel is going to allow you to deploy your Value Ladder and "funnel" your traffic through the right way.

Think creating a guided experience, online, as opposed to just letting shoppers look around on their own and leave.

Quick story to explain it.

I was sitting next to one of my mentors and good friends, Russell Brunson, working at his office in Boise on a secret project...

As I sat pondering the whole Value Ladder thing, I was struck with a bit of curiosity.

I asked Russell, "Have you ever actually ran the numbers to know how much more money a funnel makes than a standard website?"

He replied, "No, I've never thought to do that..."

Fifteen seconds later, I hear him furiously typing in a skype chat, to his main programmer, asking him to run the numbers and see.

A few minutes later, a loud scream and clapping came from just feet behind me.

It was Russell, celebrating what his programmer had messaged him back...

You probably won't believe this, like I didn't, but his programmer ran 60,000 accounts and found out that...

If.

You.

Have.

A.

Funnel.

AKA.

Your.

Value.

Ladder.

On.

The.

Internet.

Instead.

Of.

A.

Regular.

Website.

Or.

Online.

Store...

You're.

Going.

To.

Make.

514%.

MORE.

Money.

Yep, I literally gasped.

In minutes, the entire office was screaming and celebrating.

This was a very, very important piece of data...that simply illustrated in black and white the extreme opportunity that deploying a Value Ladder does for folks.

If you haven't already, it's critical to build out your own online funnel that acts as your 24/7 Value Ladder, whether you're local...global...or no matter your business.

You. Need. To. Be. Using. Funnels.

Good news!

There's software that makes this outrageously easy, like literally your buddy the Goat Farmer just drags and drops and clicks save and builds funnels that print money.

You can do it, and NEED to do it.

Unless you like NOT making 514% more money?

Go here to sign up for a FREE trial of Clickfunnels, the world's easiest funnel building software, you'll thank me later --> www.ListenToDana.com

My good friend, Russell Brunson is the co-founder. I've been using it for years and still use it every single day. We trust it with 100% of our business.

(P.S. That's my private affiliate link that you'll sign up through, and it informs Russell that you came from me...so he'll take good care of you! Don't share that link, please)

Let's dive a bit deeper and look at a real world example of me drinking my Kool-Aid...

With my pet supplements, we'd sell our anxiety relief product which, by the way, did 80% of it's annual revenue the weeks before and after the Fourth of July weekend...

We had tested the MOS offer, and found that this CO worked better...

(Hint: always test. I don't have a crystal ball, neither do you. Anybody that pretends they do, run away from.)

We tested the CO of our Bug & Pest Repellent as the upsell to our Anxiety Relief.

It looked like this:

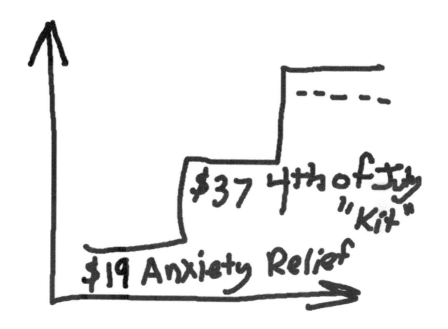

Here's another secret...

What you name your products and services REALLY matters.

We tested the straight 2 bottles of Bug & Pest Repellent as the upsell, and it converted okay.

But, when we named it the "4th of July Kit"...

It converted like crazy.

Remember, it's all about the client journey.

We know that somebody buying our Anxiety Relief on the Fourth of July would likely be doing what, next?

Taking their dogs somewhere outdoors, where there will be fireworks.

What else is outdoors?

Bugs and pests.

See how our Bug & Pest Repellent not only compliments, but enhances the results of the Anxiety Relief?

Now, there's one less thing for your dog to be anxious about.

See how easy that is?

As soon as I started mapping "Holy crap, ding, ding, ding," in my head.

That little nugget just gave you crazy awesome ideas, didn't it?

Go ahead, send goat treats to:

Billy the Goat

c/o The Derricks Group, Inc.

304 S. Jones Blvd. #1031

Las Vegas, NV 89107

^^ Billy sure appreciates it.

Another quick story.

I've got a good friend named Alex Hormozi, who is a legitimate genius and has his Value Ladder completely figured out.

No coincidence, he also has a 30-million-dollar company built in just over 2 years.

He uses this whole notion of a front end to make money on the back-end thing, REALLY well.

He took this to a new level and he's helping others to do the same, in the gym space.

One of my favorite examples of this in action is this...

Client journey.

Think about the audience he serves for a second. Gym owners, right? When somebody starts a gym, let's say that they start it from scratch, like a lot of them do.

I'm not talking franchises, picture the home-grown ones.

One of the first things they do is what? They have to cover their floor. They get into the building, whether they buy or lease.

They get the keys, open up the door, and are welcomed with a big, empty, bare building.

Most likely concrete on the floor.

What they have to do is they have to cover the floor, before they can fill it up with equipment, before they can do really anything they need to cover and protect that floor.

They've got to create a safe environment for their members, right?

One of the very first things every new gym owner does is they buy gym mats.

Remember, most companies do NOT have a Value Ladder.

So, most companies that sell gym mats do NOT have a Value Ladder.

They look like this:

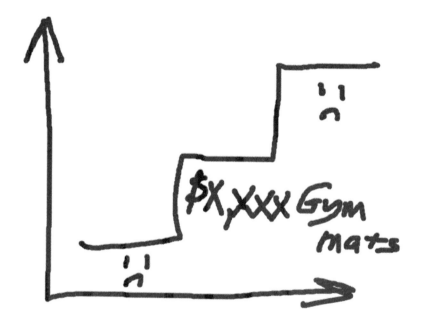

Check this out.

This is cool.

There's only a handful of suppliers of these gym mats in the United States. So, Alex very intelligently approached a few of the gym mat sellers and was able to land a few deals with them to have them send their customers his way after they buy the gym mats.

Alex would the companies selling the gym mats a nice little kickback (commission) for every time those referred customers bought Alex's program.

In other words, it looked like this:

If I buy my gym mats from Ronnie, and then Ronnie says, "Hey, by the way, you need to go check out Alex. He's going to help you monetize the crap out of your gym and run it the right way."

And then I'm like, "Oh cool." And then I enter into Alex's world, like his stuff, and invest in his program, Donnie will get a kickback or commission from Alex.

Cool, right?

Here's the real magic, though...

Ronnie, the guy selling gym mats, after a while he starts recognizing that, "Holy crap, sending my customers over to Alex is paying me a lot."

In fact, if you think about it most eCommerce businesses being just a product, not a real business.

It's not just Ronnie and gym mats.

It's everybody.

I've found myself starting not to wonder why 90% of businesses fail...but why NOT...running their business the old fashioned way, withOUT a Value Ladder.

Makes sense, doesn't it?

Ronnie used to be a product. He was gym mats, which isn't a business, but an offer.

Good news came for Ronnie, though...

Pretty soon Ronnie started making MORE money sending his customers to Alex than he was making money off of his gym mats.

Yep, how epic is THAT?

Ronnie doubled-down on this...and actually carved Alex's stuff into his Value Ladder.

It went from casually mentioning Alex's program...to literally designing his business to feed it.

Huge difference.

Guess where he's making all of his money? On the secret back-end.

Isn't that awesome?

Here's what that looks like:

Like any good entrepreneur who wants to win, Ronnie took it even further…by lowering his prices on his gym mats to the point where he's just breaking even, not even making money anymore.

He cut out his margin, and guess what happened?

Where do you think all the gyms buy their mats from?

Yep.

Value Ladder.

Client Journey.

Use this stuff.

...guess what's happening to Ronnie's competitors?

They're sitting there scratching their heads, because they have no idea what's happening and how Ronnie is able to sell these gym mats for the price he is while keeping his doors open.

Meanwhile, Ronnie's sitting there laughing his tail off because nobody even can see what's happening because it's all in the secret back-end thanks to his Value Ladder.

This is the difference between being just a product or a service, and being a business.

Who do you think is going to last longer in that market?

The ones that monetize the crap out of this back-end by way of a Value Ladder.

Here's another secret sauce behind this whole thing...

Ronnie also knows that the more people he can get to buy gym mats from him means the more eyeballs that he has on his next offer.

His next offer being Alex's offer.

Let that sink in for a minute.

I'm just tossing out numbers for illustration purposes, and have no idea if they're accurate.

I'm not in this business, but let's just for argument's sake let's say that a gym mat costs $40 per standard roll.

Now, if Ronnie keeps his price at $40, which is competitive in his market, and let's say that he acquires 10 customers a day at that price point.

That means that every day Ronnie has 10 new eyeballs that he sends over to Alex's offer to try and monetize on the back-end.

Not a terrible business.

Better than the 90% that are failing, right?

Now, how about Ronnie makes just ONE tweak to get into not the 10% he's in...but the elite 1%??

Check this out.

If Ronnie reduced his price per gym mat from $40, which was competitive and he was actually profitable, to just $20 and ends up breaking even (no profit margin)...here's what happens...

Instead of 10 orders a day, he's going to vastly increase because more folks will buy from him at $20/mat than at $40/mat.

Let's say his number of orders increases from 10 per day to 50.

Cool side effect? He's gobbling up almost all of the market.

Here's the magic.

Now, although he's not making any money on the gym mats anymore, something else that's even MORE important IS happening...

Let's say for clean, neat purposes, that all of his customers are purchasing 10 rolls of gym mats, each.

Before, remember he was pulling 10 customers per day.

If his profit margin was 50%, his profit was this:

That's $20 x 10 = $200 profit per customer.

$200 profit x 10 customers = $2,000 profit.

In other words, he was making two grand a day on these gym mats to sell to 10 customers.

Everybody else Ronnie's competing with is making about that.

Let's factor in the revenue Ronnie generates by sending his customers over to Alex.

To keep it simple, let's assume that 10% of the customers that Ronnie refers over to Alex end up buying his program...which brings a nice $2,000 commission over to Ronnie.

So, with this example, of the 10 customers Ronnie is acquiring every day...1 ends up signing up for Alex's program.

That's 10 customers x 10% conversion = 1 referred customer to Alex.

Again, the commission is $2,000 per customer, so Ronnie just landed another nice $2,000.

Doubled his daily profit.

Not bad, eh?

That's being in the 10%.

Ronnie doesn't want to be in the 10%.

Nope.

Let's get him into the 1%.

Now, Ronnie has done the unthinkable.

He's slashed the price in half.

He's making zero.

Somebody with very tight britches is getting diarrhea just thinking about this...

Ronnie went from making $2000 to $0.

Dumb, most would say.

Smart, according to the Value ladder.

Watch.

Now, instead of 10 people having eyeballs on Alex's offer, it increased to 50 a day.

Let's keep all else equal.

Here's what that looks like...

After, Ronnie's now pulling 50 customers per day.

If his profit margin is now 0%, his profit is this:

That's $0 x 50 = $0 profit per customer.

$0 profit x 50 customers = $0 profit.

Oh no.

Poor old Ronnie went from making two grand a day on these gym mats to $0...and is shipping out 5x as many ☹.

What has he done?

Now, let's factor in the revenue Ronnie generates by sending his customers over to Alex.

Again, let's assume that 10% of the customers that Ronnie refers over to Alex end up buying his program...which brings a nice $2,000 commission over to Ronnie.

So, with this example, of the now 50 customers Ronnie is acquiring every day...5 ends up signing up for Alex's program.

That's 50 customers x 10% conversion = 5 referred customers to Alex.

Again, the commission is $2,000 per customer, so Ronnie just landed not $2,000 like before...

But $10,000!!!

That's 5x his daily profit running a regular gym mat "business"...and 2.5x his daily profit before he slashed his prices and turned his gym mats into a front end offer!

BOOM!

Get your money's worth from this book, yet?

We're still just getting started 😊

Look again at the before and after.

Before, Ronnie's making two grand a day, that's it.

For somebody that doesn't know any better...they'd say he's doing really well. He's got a business.

They think the way to make more money would be to sell more gym mats.

We know better.

So does Ronnie.

Best part of all?

After, Ronnie's now making $10K a day referring folks to Alex's program on the back-end, and he doesn't even have to make any money on the gym mats.

Pressure's completely off.

Think about this.

What if YOU didn't need to make money on what you're currently selling?

Like, just letting people have it.

For much less than you're currently charging...

How much would that enable you to SLAY your competitors?

For myself, Ronnie, Trent, and everybody else that leverages a Value Ladder, we've got our "thing that sells the thing".

Ronnie's gym mats are the thing that sells Alex's program.

It's the thing that sells the thing.

With a little bit of tweaking, Ronnie could get that 10% take rate up to 20%, and guess what happens instantly?

By doing little things, like calling people, having them watch a presentation, or following up with them and listening to them then serving them, he could easily get that from 10%, the take rate from 20%+.

Guess what that does?

Instantly doubles his daily profit from $10,000 to $20,000.

AND...

Check this out.

Ronnie has ZERO fulfillment on that extra back-end money he's making.

None.

That's all in Alex's hands.

Isn't that cool?

THAT is the difference, right there, between a product and a business.

THAT is how to create a fail-proof business.

THAT is how the rich get richer.

Here's what I want you to do and start thinking about right now.

Think about your thing, whatever that is, that you currently offer or are considering offering.

Your product, service, whatever it is.

I want you to think about how and where your offer could fit into either another offer of yours or someone else's.

What we're going to do, by the end of this book, is have your Value Ladder built out the RIGHT way, by either plugging in your product and services into the gaps of other people's products and services, or fill them with your own.

Man...the clarity you're experiencing, alone, has already more than paid for whatever price you paid for this book, huh?

Keep reading.

Soon, you're going to walk out of here not with what most think is a business but isn't, but you're going to walk out of here with a real, actual, legitimate business with a fully built Value Ladder.

Epic, huh?

Get your brain rolling.

Let's say that you have a medium to high ticket thing right now.

What could you plug in front of that to help sell that?

In other words, the thing that sells your thing.

For Trent, remember, he had life insurance. Those are big contracts, good money for him.

Then he plugged in, using his Value Ladder, car insurance in front of that. That was his thing that sells his thing.

For me, I've got one of the best programs on planet Earth for entrepreneurs and called the Dream 100™ Launch Program.

Drinking my Kool-Aid, I have another book (which is actually the sequel to the book you're reading), called the Dream 100™ Book. That's my thing that sells the thing.

The cool part is you can find other people's stuff to put in front of your stuff, and let's flip it, vice versa.

Let's say that you have a lower ticket item...something inexpensive like a physical product.

Think client journey.

What can you offer next, that they need AFTER?

What's a great front end offer, that they need BEFORE?

It doesn't necessarily have to mean that you have to launch another thing.

You'll know by the end of this book what you need to plug into your Value Ladder, but which may be another person's product or service that can plug into the back of yours, just like Ronnie with his gym mats.

Ideally, we'll make more money on our back-end.

I know you want to put this book down and go jump in...but...you have to do this the right way.

Keep reading.

Every page.

It's all about the client journey and what problems they have that we can solve.

We'll build your Value Ladder, piece by piece, and by the endo of this book...you're going to have the business you dreamed of.

Let's start diving into the nuts and bolts of building this bad boy, shall we? (Don't stop reading)

Chapter #4

"Carving WHAT Into WHO Is The Only Way To Really Be In The Top 1%? (Is That Even Legal?)"

I have to be totally honest with you and fully disclose something critical. Something that most people in my position would probably be super resistant to exposing and would most likely omit...

Ya know that whole "lying by omission" thing?

Is there, "truth by extreme-honesty"?

If so, this is it.

If I lose ya, I lose ya.

I'm confident you'll like me that much more, though, for being so honest with you (I'm a farmer, remember, I can't help it)...

Here goes: to get your entire Value Ladder built out, it's not going to be easy.

In fact, it's not going to happen anytime soon.

AHHHHHHHHHHHHH...I know, I know.

I've been dangling this amazing, life-changing path to take...and now I'm telling you it's going to be difficult and take a long time...

It's like showing a cookie to a little kid, then eating it in front of them.

How cruel.

Okay, let's reel this back in and get some context.

Let me explain...

I know it sounds strange because I've been kind of selling you on the concept of the Value Ladder throughout the book and how I've even gone as far as saying "Hey, you're not a real business if you don't have one."

...to then go back and pull the rug from underneath you and then say "Well, it's really hard. And you're not going to have it done any time soon."

WHY did you do that, Dana?

I'm going to save you from potentially making a huge mistake. That's why.

Here's what I mean....

Crap.

Printer running out of ink again.

If you want me to continue, send a bag of money to:

Billy the Goat

c/o The Derricks Group, Inc.

304 S. Jones Blvd. #1031

Las Vegas, NV 89107

Just kidding.

Send 2 bags. 😉

Okay, fine.

Here's the costly, tragic mistake…

Most people think they know what a Value Ladder is, but don't.

I've mentioned before that I was introduced to this concept by one of my really good friends, Russell Brunson, and it changed my life.

It's fantastic.

By the way, if you haven't read his book DotCom Secrets, yet, you need to read that.

Then, sign up for Clickfunnels so you can implement this like crazy --> www.ListenToDana.com (unless you hate money)

Thank me later.

Now, here's the deal and why lots of folks get this wrong.

Is it cool if I just give you one of the biggest nuggets that you've ever gotten in your life?

Ready?

Check this out… a normal, basic Value Ladder, looks something like this…

(Credit Russell Brunson for inspiring this, btw)

As you can see, most businesses will be able to pull that off.

The simple, old Value Ladder.

Over time, they'll have a front end with cheap, free stuff to get folks into the door.

Then, more expensive stuff on the back.

Pretty simple.

Basic.

Old.

Outdated.

Not how you can absolutely dominate and REALLY put your dent in the world, though...

Let me show you what that's missing.

Take a peek at the cover of this book, see how there's another side to the Value Ladder that extends back down?

What most people think is a Value Ladder is only HALF of one.

To have a fully built out Value Ladder, and to complete your business, there actually is a back side to it.

Like this.

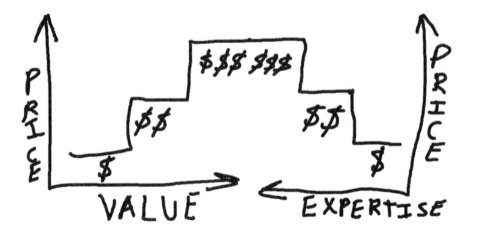

When you have the first half of your Value Ladder built out...
something really cool happens.

You're actually creating a demand for something else.

For example, let's say that you have an online course or
coaching program that helps people to become something
new.

Let's say that your course was to help people to be a better
salesperson.

All right, cool.

Your program helps them be a better salesperson.

Now, what you've just created, though, is a demand on the
other side of your value ladder that you probably don't even
realize exists...

You created a really good salesperson in your program, right?

Well, there's a huge group of folks out there that'd LOVE to
have that salesperson join their team, wouldn't they?

There's a demand for salespeople, and a HUGE demand for
good ones.

What should you do about that?

YOU should not just create the demand...but ALSO fulfill the supply.

In other words, you need to then fill in on the back side of your Value Ladder.

How?

Ready for this?

Certify your students.

Have a certification program on the back side.

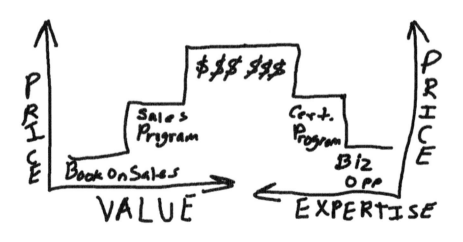

When your student comes through your course, or your program, on the front side of the Value Ladder, the good ones will do well, obviously.

AND...there are people out there that want to hire the good ones.

Here's why that's absolutely magical, for you.

1) You can instantly discern a good one from a bad one by plugging them into a certification program

2) You get paid to do that

They pay you to show them how to become a better salesperson...they pay you to certify them...

Happily pay you, by the way.

And then what do you do?

At the top of the back side of your Value Ladder, you hand over those certified people over to the people that want to hire them.

Guess what.

You get paid, AGAIN.

You should charge a fee for that, as well.

At the very top right of your Value Ladder, you should have a done-for-you (agency type) offer built out at the top.

There will ALWAYS be folks that just want to dump money at people to do it for them.

Big money.

I see this with 5 and 6-figure copywriting jobs all the time.

So, on the front of your Value Ladder, it could very well be just a DIY (do it yourself) or DWY (done with you), like going through your Sales Program.

But, on the back side, it should be full blown DFY (done for you).

Like this.

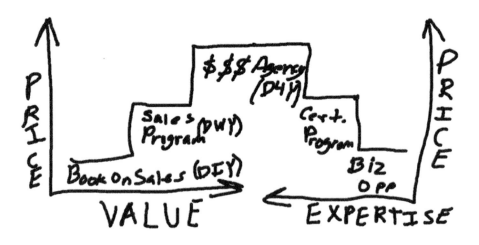

If you've got somebody that wants to pay you a hundred thousand dollars, a million dollars, whatever, your company should take that money, right?

Otherwise, they're going to give it to someone else.

So, the best people that go through your certification program, you can either let other companies hire them and be the connector (charging a fee)...OR you can simply keep them for yourself and use them on your own team...either for your own internal company projects or for clients (e.g. agency).

Pretty cool the possibilities, huh?

Essentially, you're creating a marketplace...and controlling ALL of it.

You own the entire town.

The apartment they live in, the grocery store they shop at, the diner they eat at, everything.

...and they LOVE you for it, because your town is WAY better than the other towns.

In other words, you can either let others fulfill the supply to the demand that you're creating, or you can do it by way of building out your Value Ladder completely.

Which option do you think's going to build you a more rock-solid business?

Which option do you think is going to make you a ton more money and help you serve WAY more people?

Which option do you think is going to skyrocket the value of your business for when you go to sell it?

Here's the coolest part.

You can actually enroll people into your certification program for your thing as a new opportunity, AKA a "business opportunity" or "biz opp".

Check this out...

Let's go back to the example of selling a program or course on selling.

For most, selling the course and program on selling would make sense to be sold to an existing salesperson that wants to get better at their craft, right?

Sure.

However...look at what that's missing.

There are a TON of people out there who are "stuck" in existing opportunities that are leaving much to be desired and want OUT, right?

Think folks working a 9-5.

...or folks that are exploring other opportunities that just aren't turning out to be what they were promised (e.g. network marketing, real estate, etc.).

THOSE people would DIE for an awesome opportunity to make more money doing something more enjoyable than what they're currently doing.

So, they're PERFECT candidates to BECOME a killer salesperson from whatever they currently are.

Sally may be a hairdresser this week, but she could be a stone-cold salesperson next week by going through your program.

Trevor is sick of being a personal trainer and wants to do something from home, so he could do phone closes right from home after going through your program.

See how many people out there NEED our stuff, but we have to be creative about how we position it and offer it?

Thank you, Value Ladder, for giving us the formula!

Simply putting those folks into our program, then certifying them, as they climb our Value Ladder will produce the supply, naturally!

Boom!

By now, you can tell that a real Value Ladder is more than just a simple little, "Oh yeah, I get it Dana, you just send someone into the next thing."

No.

Like, to have a completed business, you need your entire Value Ladder built out to control the entire ecosystem, okay?

That way, you'll control both the supply and the demand, and you make money every possible way...plus service everybody to the fullest. It's amazing.

Here's the deal.

I know what you're thinking. "Okay, Dana, that is amazing, and I can see the vision for my business, but this is going to take years to build the right way."

And it absolutely will, okay?

Full disclosure: I'm still building mine.

BUT...there's a fast forward button.

Ready for that?

You want to know how to build out your ENTIRE Value Ladder the RIGHT Way, both sides of it, withOUT spending a decade doing it?

You ready for this?

You can actually fast forward to get your Value Ladder Built Out by leveraging other people's products or.

Just like Ronnie the gym mat seller using my friend Alex's program to build the top of his Value Ladder, quickly.

HOW, though?

You'll use this thing called The Dream 100™ Strategy where you find other people that have amazing products or services that would fit your value ladder...

...then you can, essentially, co-brand, co-partner with and have other people's products and services fill out your entire Value Ladder, and get it done in days instead of years!

Isn't that awesome?

Laying out that strategy deserves a book of it's own, and you will NOT want to try to do this on your own...

So, if you don't already have a copy of the Award-Winning Dream 100™ Book, head over to --> www.Dream100Book.com/free

Grab a copy, inhale it, it will change your life.

Also, if you haven't already joined the Dream 100™ Challenge, do that unless you hate money --> www.Dream100Challenge.com

Instead of filling this book to 600 pages...I've put those resources together for you to literally walk you through the entire process of finding your Dream 100™, identifying who your Dream 100™ is, how to get their contact info, what to say to them, how to monetize the relationship, and it's all just done for you (you just fill in the blanks and press go).

Again, that's the only way to get your Value Ladder built the right way...withOUT spending years.

Although I haven't built both sides of my Value Ladder with my own products and services, I HAVE built it completely with my Dream 100™ Partner's products and services.

...but here's where it gets way cooler, here's the real gold.

You ready for this?

Other people are building their Value Ladders with ME and MY products built into it.

Guess what that does?

It pumps out new customers to me, every single day, for FREE...

Yep, I have carved my thing into their thing.

As a result, I get literally gobs and gobs of FREE customers and leads every single day because of that.

Just like Alex.

That's the power of the Dream 100™.

THAT'S the side of the Value Ladder YOU want to be on.

Now that's awesome, right?

That's why I wrote an entire book on the subject, and why you need to start NOW (don't wait).

Let's wrap this chapter up and to get you thinking the right way.

One of the many strategies I lay out and break down inside the Dream 100™ Challenge is the concept of integrating, or carving your thing into other people's things.

After all, if somebody out there doesn't have a really expensive thing, and your thing is really expensive, they should put your expensive thing in their Value Ladder so they're pushing everybody to your thing...which makes them more money.

Carving other folks into your Value Ladder is great to temporarily build it out, but you want to be on the receiving end of folks carving YOU into THEIR Value Ladder as much as possible.

^^ THAT is infinitely scaleable (if you can keep up with the demand, of course)

You may only have room for 1-2 people to carve into your Value Ladder, like this:

On the other side...

You've got INFINITE room for others to carve you into THEIR Value Ladder, like this:

"O.P.O." in this example standing for "Other People's Offer".

See how other people's offer can fit perfectly as the front end to YOUR Value Ladder...and how dang quickly you can blow things up?

Here's the formula to success:

Value Ladder + Dream 100™ = BOOM

That's it.

Again, Ronnie the gym mat seller is just ONE example of somebody sending his customers over to Alex's Value Ladder.

He's got COUNTLESS others doing the exact same.

Software for fitness pros.

Supplement suppliers.

Equipment vendors.

The list goes on.

Okay, okay...

If you're sitting there thinking, "Okay, Dana...that's great for somebody that sells high-ticket. I have something that's not even close to that."

You're in luck.

If you sell something that's not really expensive...here's how you'll Dream 100™ it...

The FAST way is you'll find somebody that DOES has an expensive offer, and then send your people to them, instead of building it out.

You can still be on the receiving end of folks pushing their customers to your Value Ladder...by just mapping out your client's journey and figuring out what's happening BEFORE they need your product/service...

Here's what's cool, and a couple practical ways to do that.

(Again, this is something I map out for you and give you tools to quickly implement inside the Dream 100™ Challenge in Module #2).

This, on it's own, is going to change your business forever.

Think of it this way.

Walt Disney is a very interesting person, and one of the best entrepreneurs to ever live.

He was very hardcore.

Most people know him for the Mickey Mouse stuff, but a few of us know him the way that he really was...the insane business man.

He had a rule.

He would go to Disney World, and would literally walk around the park seeing if his rule was broken.

He'd discreetly "test" everyone in his whole company.

He called it his "ten step rule".

If you could walk ten steps without having the opportunity to buy something, the rule was broken.

Walt would show up, unannounced, and absolutely flip out if his rule was broken.

At Disney World, you'll notice this to this day still a rule.

Go and try it, you can't get ten steps without the ability to buy something. Literally.

Everything is for sale everywhere.

And the cool thing is, we can emulate that, and that's all I do is I emulate Walt's rule.

Every ten steps, how can someone buy something?

That doesn't mean we're forcing our products and services down people's throats, we're just giving them the ability to give us money.

No different than the 514% more money, thing, using a sales funnel (Value Ladder on the internet) as opposed to the old fashioned way.

I drink my Kool-Aide, by the way.

...one place that I've been doing this is by attaching my Dream 100™ Book to other people's checkout pages.

"Oh, you bought Tim's blah blah? Great, you also unlocked a copy of the Dream 100™ Book! Go here to claim it"

Ten steps.

Every time somebody else on my Dream 100™ acquires a customer they're sent to that checkout page.

Are they selling anything on that page?

Almost nobody is.

Which violates Walt's rule.

So, I go ahead and I fix that for them, because I plug in my Dream 100™ Book into it, and it solves their problem of not monetizing that page, and basically letting their customer go down the road without an opportunity to buy something right then and there.

It also helps me, because now I get to acquire 100% FREE leads and customers all day long like crazy.

I don't have to pay any money to be on that page, I just give them a commission whenever somebody buys my book, it's like FREE advertising for me.

So that's one really cool place.

Also live events, like getting my book into the hands of the people that attend the live event, either by distributing it ahead of time so it's in the welcome bag or whatever.

Also, not too long ago I had a booth as a vendor and gave away books, so I worked my books into live events as much as I can.

Membership areas.

I create a bonus module for folks as they go through other people's courses, and I get them back into my world and my Value Ladder.

You've likely seen this happening in the mail, before.

If you receive purchase something that's going to be mailed to you, a lot of times you'll notice that there are other flyers for other things inside of it.

That's an awesome way to penetrate someone else's Value Ladder to bring their customer back over to yours.

Again, the real gold is carving your thing into other people's Value Ladder with the Dream 100™.

As you can see, there's literally endless amounts of opportunity to leverage other people's offers to build your Value Ladder, and vice versa.

You can probably tell that the best, most lucrative thing you can possibly do is to deploy the Dream 100™ to get other people to carve your offer into their Value Ladder.

I'll prove it.

Think of the guy that sells the gym mats, Ronnie, he can't promote 75 different people's programs to the people that buy his gym mats...because that just would be weird.

It would pull people all over the place and wouldn't be effective.

Think of the other way around, though.

Alex CAN have way more than just the one person promoting/prescribing his stuff, right? Building his stuff into others' Value Ladder naturally pushes people back over to him.

That's literally as simple as it is. It doesn't need to be more complicated, it's not.

To build your entire Value Ladder the right way, that's what you need.

...and if you don't want to build your entire Value Ladder right now (which you shouldn't even try, by the way), just find someone else's stuff, follow and use my tools and resources inside the Dream 100™ Challenge, and then, BAM!

Your Value Ladder is built and pumping out unlimited leads and customers!!!

Up next I'm going to show you the ONLY way you should look at your offer...and why selling is NOT the way to make a lot of money (I know, that doesn't make any sense...or does it?).

Keep reading.

Chapter #5

"The 4 'Silent Poisons' Of EVERY Business...And How A Stubborn Old Football Coach Found The Antidote..."

We are really rolling now. I mean, come on. Aren't we? Let's turn it up a notch...

There's ONE thing you need to do if you want to have success with everything I'm laying out to you...

Which, incidentally, is also something you need to do if you just want to do well in business...

Here it is.

If you want to make MORE money than you thought imaginable...

You need to STOP selling.

Yep, I know that sounds weird. "Dana, how am I going to be successful or make money if I don't sell?"

Fair question.

Here's what I mean.

The days of the "me to you" style selling are really, really dwindling.

That's the old model.

It's dying.

Why?

People suck, and have under delivered and over promised for way too long.

Remember, we live in a world where the commercial for the burger is not what you are going to receive when you show up, right?

Not even close.

That style of selling is just not working anymore.

Instead, we're going to stop selling, we're just going to stop selling the thing directly.

Look at all the companies that are crazy successful.

They typically don't sell the thing directly.

They sell the thing that sells the thing.

That's all we're doing differently.

So again, think of my friend Trent, he doesn't sell life insurance. Why?

Because everybody else is fighting to sell life insurance.

He sells the car insurance auto policy, so that he can sell the life insurance.

More importantly, he builds that relationship and trust, first.

Let's take that a step further...

In case you're not entirely sure WHAT exactly should be your "thing that sells the thing", let's get super clear.

Instead of just jumping into building something that we THINK is going to be the perfect "thing that sells the thing"...

...we need to get clear on ONE thing.

What's the preferred method of consumption for our customer or client avatar?

This. Is. Critical.

Here's what I mean by that.

One of the biggest offenders of well-intended yet ignorant marketing, is...ready for it?

A webinar.

For some reason, everybody thinks they need a webinar.

So, everybody's building a webinar, creating a webinar, or at least has a webinar on their to-do list.

Let's break this down, for a second...

By the way, let me preface what I'm about to drop on you by saying that I've personally done hundreds of webinars, so I'm not saying they're useless.

Not at all.

Check this out.

WHY was a webinar originally invented?

Simple reason.

Because somebody had a great problem.

They had a problem that the webinar solved.

WHAT was the problem?

They had WAY too many leads or customers to try and sell something to, so they needed to be able to "mass sell" to them.

No different than why schools have busses that carry 53 passengers instead of minivans that carry 7.

It's a fantastic problem.

I'll take that problem all day long.

BUT, that was the point of the webinar.

If you analyze this historically, the most effective webinars are the ones that have the most people on them, right?

That's kind of the point.

The most successful schools have full school busses and classrooms.

With that being said...

I have seen people misuse webinars left and right.

There are GOBS of people out there building webinars that have ZERO audience.

It's so bad, they don't even have one person that will watch the webinar.

I'm just like, "Okay, well why are you building that?".

It's no different than a school buying a fleet of full size busses to only put a handful of kids on them.

Not smart.

Forehead slap.

Here's what's even worse...

They don't bother to stop and think about if a webinar is even their avatar's preferred method of consumption, anyway...

I don't watch webinars.

I'm not everybody, but if somebody wants to sell me something...I won't be buying it if they're trying to use a webinar as their thing that sells the thing.

Nope.

Here's a glaring example that somebody paid me $25,000 to find out...

I had a client fly out to my office to do a private consulting day with me. We were chatting about who his customer avatar is, and figuring out how he was targeting them.

He suggested that his avatar was CEOs.

By the way, this guy is awesome. His stuff is REALLY good and he's a sharp guy, but he was just not getting quality leads...

He couldn't put his finger on it.

He kept saying he thought he needed to tweak his webinar and messaging, because he just couldn't manage to get folks to show up. Worse, those that did just weren't buying.

I confidently said, "Okay, this one's easy. We're going to solve this and then have time to feed the goats."

I asked him, "So who's your avatar, again?"

"CEOs", he replied.

I ask him, "Okay, cool...and what exactly have you been doing to reach them at this point? What's your thing that sells the thing?"

He said, "A webinar."

I'm like, "Are CEOs watching webinars? Are they consuming webinars?"

He thinks about it for a few seconds. "No, I wouldn't think they'd spend 90 minutes on a webinar..."

I reply, "Okay, cool. We've established that, so let's not reinvent the wheel.

Let's leverage what you've already created with a webinar.

I'm not telling you that we have to throw that away and start from scratch, but what ARE they consuming? Like HOW are they consuming information?"

...he looks at me, perplexed.

"Well, what's the biggest badge of honor every CEO always brags about, and other people even brag about, that they credit the CEO with being as successful as they are because of it? What is the one thing they always brag about?", I ask, as I point to the pile of a dozen of my books I've authored on the conference table...

"They always brag about how many books they read. They read a book a week, on average. 52 in a year."

I see the wheels spinning in his head.

He's battling the "holy-crap-Dana-just-laid-the-truth-on-me" feeling...mixed with the "I've-been-doing-it-all-wrong-but-that-means-I've-been-lied-to"...which is perfectly normal, mind you.

I'm like, "Do you think that you should be running webinars, or do you think you should have a book? Let's put your webinar into a book, and then let's target CEOs with your book. How's that? Because that's how they consume information."

Instead of trying to drag a CEO onto a webinar for 90 minutes...just give them what they're already doing...a book!

He replies, "Ding, Ding, Ding, Ding, Ding!"

He left the room to call his business partner, then wife.

"We've got to turn the webinar into a book", he shouted excitedly on both calls.

I sat there, sipped my sparkling water, grinning from ear to ear.

Of course, I helped him get his book done, so he could get it in the hands of CEO's. He followed my same exact system that's helped me to author over 12 books.

Good ones, too.

If you want to get YOUR book done, so you have a "thing that sells the thing", just go over to the Author Challenge --> www.AuthorChallenge.com

You'll get your DREAM book done in a week instead of 10 years, and for about 5% the cost you'd spend with a traditional publisher. Every single piece of it from extracting it from your brain, to putting it all into a perfectly progressive outline and frame, to editing/formatting, to design, to printing, fulfillment, etc.

No stone unturned and you can use the same system over and over and over.

In fact, that's exactly what Tucker, from Salt Lake City did.

Using the Author Challenge, he's got 2 of his own books that are his "thing that sells the thing" to blow the lid off of his agency...plus his wife has gotten her book done to do the same with her small business!

Your turn.

Anyway, since that consulting session, you guessed it.

My client launched his book and is DESTROYING.

He's got way more leads than he can handle, as CEOs are all going bonkers for his book.

Simple little tweak of making his "thing that sells the thing" into the way that THEY want to consume information.

I get it.

It might not be as clear for you when you are creating your thing that sells your thing, or if you already have, as to how people are going to consume it.

There's SO much out there it can be maddening to know exactly which direction to go.

For me, for example, like with that CEO it's clear they read books. Duh.

Sometimes, I honestly don't know if my customers are reading, listening, or watching.

In fact, I have no clue if you're reading this book or listening to my lovely voice read it to you.

So, I just give you both.

As you noticed, I sell the book, but also I give the audio version away for free.

I also give out lots of new, lots of video, as well.

However I can get my customer to consume it, is what matters most.

This is where I differ with some people. Some people will sell the audio version of their book as like an upsell or a bonus on top of the actual physical copy. I will never do that.

I always give it away. Why?

Because I don't want to deprive someone of an opportunity to consume my thing that sells my things.

There we go.

Drinking my Kool-Aide.

That just makes sense that way, doesn't it?

Somebody might buy my book, but not the audio version, and then they may not ever read it.

It might sit on their shelf and collect dust.

At least they have a chance to listen to it if they get busy or are stuck at an airport.

So, yeah, stop selling your thing directly, and start selling your thing that sells the thing...and in the format that your customer avatar is already consuming.

That'll work much better than anything else you could do, trust me.

Next, let's pile on something else that you should NOT do in order to have success.

Please, just don't do this.

Another thing I see people trying to do is getting really fancy with their marketing.

They try to build a million things at once.

Of course, I'm guilty of this, too...but what they'll do is they just try to get way too fancy. And what ends up happening is it just becomes kind of a distraction and causes confusion.

As you know, the more confused someone is, the less likely they are going to buy.

Or consume something.

Right now, less is more.

Simple is the new sexy.

Quick story.

I was doing some consulting work for a program that caters to gym owners.

Like the quality control freak that I am, I actually physically went in a couple of their facilities and posed as a customer.

I always wanted to be a mystery shopper, as a kid. This was my chance.

The gym owner and the gym trainer met me, and had no idea. I posed as if I was going to join their gym so I could walk through the whole process of their onboarding and their enrolling.

I remember of the two gyms I visited, one was doing pretty well and the other wasn't.

My primary goal was to compare and contrast between the two and figure out why, because neither of them had a lead problem.

The problem was that one wasn't enrolling as many as the other.

I quickly diagnosed what was going on, and the difference between the two...and we were able to fix this and then standardize it across all of the gyms.

...and then it was like BAM! Everybody in the program got better results.

Wanna know what the problem was?

I'm not sure I can tell you...

I haven't seen that bag of money, yet?

Ha.

For realz.

You don't have to send me a bag of money.

Just buy all my stuff.

After all, it's kinda like hitting a heater on a slot machine at the casino.

You put $XXX in, and get $X,XXX out...

Or, you put $XX,XXX in, and get $XXX,XXX or $X,XXX,XXX out.

Deal? ☺

Okay...well the problem was NOT that one gym was better than the other.

Or that one owner was smarter, friendlier, or had better people skills than the other.

Or that one was newer, bigger, or played cooler music.

Nope.

Ready for this?

One of the gyms, when they made the offer to join, was really confusing.

On a single sheet of paper, which was handed to me as I walked out the door, there was:

> A fitness challenge I could sign up for with two options (6-week and 12-week)

> A standard membership option

> An upgraded membership level

> A one-time fee for something like a consultation (I think?)

> ...and something else I can't quite remember

I remember, on my way out, stopping the gym owner in the lobby and saying, "Okay, if I join the challenge am I a member, or am I just in the challenge? Does that give me access to everything? And then what's that fee? Is that only if I sign up today?"

Without a thorough, time-consuming explanation, I couldn't easily understand what the difference was between any of it, and the sheet did NOT explain it.

Bottom line: there was just way too much on there.

Contrast that with the other gym, the one that was doing well.

Their offer sheet was very simple.

It had:

> Membership option a: 3 days per week large group training

> Membership option b: 4 days per week small group training + nutrition accountability

It was, "Here are our two membership options. Which one looks better to you?"

And I'm like, "All right, this makes sense. This is why you're doing really well, and the other one's not."

We like to overcomplicate things, sometimes, and it's just not necessary.

Less really is more.

Not having a thing that sells your thing...will kill your business.

Folks not consuming your thing...will kill your business.

Confusing your potential customers...will kill your business.

Want to know what the WORST way for your business to die, is?

(I know, this is awfully cynical, isn't it? Well, the whole point of this book is to deep-dive on why 90% of businesses all die a miserable death...so...there's that)

One of the worst things I see (which doubles as the best way to kill a business) is this.

They stop doing the things that got them to where they are.

I forbid you from stopping yourself from doing the things that you did to get you to where you are.

Here's what I mean.

When a sports team makes a playoff run, a lot of times you'll see some teams that were very highly rated and who a lot of people thought were going to do really well.

They absolutely crumble and "choke" in the playoffs. Eliminated right away. Round one.

They get "upset" by a team that shouldn't have beat them, at least on paper.

Probably cost a lot of people some big money.

Good thing I don't gamble. I'm terrible at it.

Most times, it's just simply that is due to the simple fact that they stopped doing the things that they were doing that, you know, got them there.

Here's a practical example.

They may have stopped practicing every morning, or their practice routine got screwed up, or they started eating crappy food, or they weren't doing enough film sessions, or they got thrown off of their routine, and they stopped doing the little things.

Those little things were what they did to get them to where they are. And as a result, what happens? They get beat, right?

That's why it really is critically important to identify the things that you're doing now that are contributing to the success that you're having, even if it's nominal.

And then continue to do those.

Run that play.

I'm not lying when I say it's not the sexy things that make us money, or that we do well from.

I'll prove it.

Back in high school, I had a legend for a football coach, coach Adler. Awesome dude.

His grandson was on my team, so we were lucky enough to have him come out of his coaching retirement to help coach us.

Before him, our team was terrible.

Coach Adler was a high profile coach, an inductee of the high school coaching hall of fame and everything. He came back and he took us to, I believe, five undefeated conference championships...starting year 1 and ending with his retirement after year 5.

5-for-5.

Incredible...

It was huge, huge turn around.

One of the main reasons that he had so much success was his stubbornness.

I'm not kidding.

I'll never forget this story.

It perfectly describes why we had success and why the way he did things worked so well (and why you need to emulate this in your business).

We're in the middle of the game; we've got the ball. Our fullback had just gotten about five yards on a very basic run play off the right side.

I remember catching my breath, I had just laid an incredible block that left the defender flying 35 feet. Just kidding. It was 36 feet and I wasn't out of breath.

For real, though.

I'm in the huddle, listening for the next play call.

All of a sudden, instead of the normal voice of our quarterback explaining what the next play was, we hear a grown man screaming at top of his lungs from our sideline.

All of us in the huddle are stunned, and look over...

Coach Adler screamed so loud that our sideline heard it, us on the field heard it, the other team on the field heard it, the other team's sideline and coaches heard it, and I believe the entire stadium heard it.

He screamed, twice, "Run it again!"

The first time, we all stood there, deer in the headlights...

We'd never fathomed the possibility of telling the opposing team what play we would run.

Let alone screaming that we were about to run the exact same play again, loud enough that the opposing team knew it was coming, and their coaches and fans knew it was coming.

WHY did he do that?

Like Walt Disney, Coach Adler had a rule...

His rule was, simply, that if we could get five yards or more on a play, we will run that play again until they stop us.

Guess what.

We would STEAMROLL teams by running the same play over and over and over.

I know.

That makes sense, right?

Mathematically.

Like you run the numbers and if you could get five yards or more, every play, you're going to score every time barring a fumble or interception. Right?

It's just math, not magic.

And win we did.

For five straight years.

...and all these years later, that story still sticks with me.

Here's the moral.

It's not the sexy, shiny stuff that matters.

Can you imagine how boring it was to watch that game?

Right?

Same play.

Over and over and over.

That's why people don't do it.

Watching the same play over and over is terribly boring.

Even worse. Imagine coaching that game?

Terribly boring.

Or, heck, imagine playing that game!

Terribly boring. Right?

That's why folks don't keep running the same play, because it's boring.

You know this already, but it's the boring, not sexy, flashy stuff that actually contributes to us doing really well.

I hope to goodness that makes more sense now.

The good news, for you, is even though most people think that they need like this new sexy thing to succeed, they don't. You know that already.

In reality, people just need a Value Ladder that solves problems on their client journey...and the Dream 100™ to fill it.

That's it.

Literally, that's all people need.

Probably why I've made a million dollars or more in every business you can think of.

I think it's time to go NEXT LEVEL on this, if you're cool with that?

Let's go through WHAT should be on each rung of your Value Ladder...

Basically, it's your customer or client journey.

This is one of my little secrets that I use a lot: all you're doing is solving problems.

Your service or product exists and your business exists because it solves a problem.

If it doesn't, make some changes IMMEDIATELY.

It might be a good problem that it solves, but it MUST solve a problem.

Again, problems don't go away, they just change.

I remember figuring that out back when I was really broke. Back then, I thought that if I made a bunch of money, all my problems go away.

Well, I made a bunch of money and then a lot of my problems did go away. I didn't have the stress of bills, anymore.

That that went away.

Super cool feeling.

However, I had new problems that came, and they were just different.

They weren't necessarily worse.

Here's an example.

For the first time in my life, this year, I purchased a brand new SUV. Never bought a brand-new vehicle ever.

That's great.

My family has something that's safe that they're traveling in, which was a huge relief and solved problem.

BUT...it caused a new problem.

You ready for this?

Now I have to be very, very careful about where we park. We usually can't park close to other vehicles because we don't want people bashing into our new SUV.

Cue the violin and sad music.

That's an AWESOME problem, right? Heck yeah.

I'll take that problem all day long.

Different, better problem, but still a problem.

That's why valet parking was created.

To solve that problem.

Catching on, now?

Think about your client journey, right now...

Your product or your service is going to solve a problem for them.

BUT...it'll also create a new problem.

That's the cool thing.

THAT is how you get clear on what to offer them next.

For example, watch this customer journey and how problems are both solved and created...

I used to work with a lot of eCommerce businesses, did a lot of consulting and services for them.

I remember giving one of my clients a huge "aha moment" when he was all over the board with all these different products he had launched across away too many different niches...

I was like, "Ah man. Think of it a bit differently. Your business and all your products, all they do is solve the next problem. That's all it does. Okay. And here's how you know what you should be offering, or who you should partner with. Think about your customer's journey."

One of the products the guy sold was marshmallow skewers.

Like those little wooden things that you put your marshmallows on when you roast them by the campfire. Or poke your spouse with cause it's kind of funny.

I said, "Okay, you are trying to make money with these marshmallow skewers, which is fine. However, the margins are terrible and there's lots in competition, right? Like there's not much there. I wouldn't bank on these skewers making you rich. So instead, why not think of it this way.

Someone that buys marshmallow skewers, what's that going to cause them to do, next?"

My client replied, "Well, it's going to cause them the new problem of, 'Hey, we're going camping, do we have enough chairs for everybody to roast around the fire?"

Good problem.

They need chairs to make these camping memories in.

I suggested, "So, you should probably sell them camping chairs too, right? And then what does solving that problem now cause? Well they're going to get tired. They're going to need to sleep, aren't they? Okay, cool. So maybe you should sell them tents or sleeping bags, too."

See how we're filling up their Value Ladder, the smart way?

Not done.

All right, we've got them their skewers which solved the problem of not being able to make smores...

...but caused the problem of needing to be able to sit around the fire...

...which the chairs solved but caused the problem of getting sleeping and cold by being out too late...

...which the sleeping bag and tent solved...

Following me?

Now, what problem they have?

They wake up and they're like, "Oh, my back is sore. That was not a good night's sleep. I don't want to do a tent anymore. We need to do something different."

Sweet.

New problem.

Well, now what do you sell them?

Well, you should probably solve that problem by offering them a camper.

Sick.

We've gone from a few dollars on the skewers all the way up to a 5-figure purchase.

Thank you, Value Ladder ☺

Cool, now their back is feeling better but they have a new problem...

They're like, "Ah, we love this camping thing, but like, our family's too big. We want to go big. Like we want a motor home."

Oh, snap.

It's getting big-time, now.

Let's rumble.

THAT is how you turn a marshmallow skewer buyer into a Class A Motorhome buyer, with a Value Ladder.

Go back to the Dream 100™ Strategy for a second...let's dump rocket fuel on this bad boy.

Remember, you don't have to be in the motor home business to build this out.

Dream 100™ it, find someone else that IS in that business, and get a commission for sending your leads that way.

I had to scoop my client's jaw off the floor when I left him with, "You're not in the marshmallow skewer business. You are in the camping business. Your marshmallow skewers are your thing that sells the thing."

Let me just stop you for a second, k?

You're not even a third of the way through this book...and it's FLIPPING EPIC...isn't it?

Here's the deal.

If you stop reading now...

You're soft.

You're fragile.

You're not cut out to be an entrepreneur.

You can feed your dog in the morning.

You can take your spouse out next weekend.

You can sleep when you're dead.

Just. Keep. Reading.

Don't kill this momentum and get soft, now.

Coach Adler would get on your ass.

Keep reading.

Chapter #6

"The 'Sketchy Guru Lie' Exposed! Plus A Lesson On Why You Need To Point Your Burger A Certain Way Before Eating It..."

Now that your brain has been pleasantly refreshed with real, tangible gold...it's soon going to be functioning in a completely different than before you picked up this book. Pretty cool, right?

Let's double-down again on a critical piece of making this work...

This all hinges on knowing, extraordinarily well, your client or customer journey.

Not what seems to make sense when you think about it, but what they actually BUY.

In other words, that means you've got to get really laser clear on what the heck you're offering, and when, which dictates where it falls on your Value Ladder.

When you can put your pieces and fill in your Value Ladder with what you already have built, and then fill in the gaps with you need to include from your Dream 100™, THAT'S when you'll have a real, sustainable, fail-proof business.

Before we get into it...I do have to warn you about the biggest roadblock I see folks getting stuck behind...

I used to call it information overload, which I'm sure you can relate to?

So many books to read...videos to watch...podcasts to listen to...courses to go through...events to attend.

It's maddening, isn't it?

I would even go as far as saying that, worse than those feelings, is the misconception that we need make things complicated in order to work.

I said it before, but it's definitely worth expanding upon...

Here's a problem and I hate to, I mean I never intended for this book to expose of a lot of the bad stuff that goes on, but let me just share a quick bit of reality.

I've said in the past I've not been afraid of calling out certain tactics that certain people do in order to get you to consume and buy their stuff....and this one's no different.

I call it like it is.

Got that from my dad.

If you're going to do something shady to me, I'm not afraid to be honest and tell the truth.

Here's what I mean.

So, one tactic or trick that folks will use is in order to get you to buy, is to keep you confused.

Yep.

I'll prove it.

Imagine that if you knew exactly what you needed, and you really understood not only the problem but also the solution.

Would you need to go spend money and hire people?

No.

I don't understand how the engine of my car all fits together and what parts do what.

I pop the hood and get confused.

That's why I pay a mechanic.

If I knew everything they knew, I wouldn't need them.

Right?

That's an innocent example, of course.

Here's where it takes a turn and why we need to be extremely careful...

There's a group out there that intentionally keeps us confused so that we keep getting pulled and dragged into different directions and we keep buying.

You'll believe that in a second, stick with me.

A perfect example of that is, essentially, the entire weight loss market.

In the last 40 years, there hasn't really been a giant breakthrough in the way the human body works, has there? I mean, we're still eating and drinking from our mouths...still needing to sleep...still walking on two legs...all that good stuff.

Not much has changed.

...and, we also know, generally, what foods are or aren't good for us.

Sugary soda probably isn't that good.

Broccoli probably is pretty good.

Right?

Not that crazy or difficult.

BUT...the problem that keeps happening is we keep getting overloaded with information which overwhelms us and, even worse, over-complicates things...causing confusion.

How?

Well, think about it.

Let's look at, for example, the Keto diet.

Say you want to start the Keto diet but don't know a ton about it or where to start.

A quick online search will find you five articles from very credible sources, doctors sometimes, screaming the Keto diet's praises. Right?

But then, you dig a little deeper...and the next five articles, also from credible sources, and even sometimes doctors, will say that the Keto diet is the devil. Right?

Like, what the heck am I supposed to believe?

Ever felt that way?

I know you might be going through that or feeling that way with your business...and you're feeling like there's a ton more to this than you anticipated, which is understandable.

Just know that you'll be all right.

Follow my lead, I've been right where you are.

Even if that means that you wasted a little bit of time going through some stuff that you now realize, looking back, wasn't really very good.

There aren't mistakes, just lessons.

The good news?

You know now how and where to discern and to spend your time appropriately.

^^ That's freaking valuable.

Those days are over.

There's no "illusion of progress" or "intentional confusion" with me.

Just straight up value.

Here's what I want you to do right now.

I want you to list out in your mind everything that you currently have for sale, okay?

Then we're going to fill in your own Value Ladder for your entire line of products or services, soon.

Even if you don't have everything already figured out, we're going to make it happen.

So, whether you have a physical product, service, whatever, I want you to fill out potentially what your Value Ladder will be (and if you don't have everything right now for sale, that's okay, leave it blank and we'll fill those in later with our Dream 100™).

Head over to www.ValueLadderChallenge.com and take the 100% FREE Challenge to fill up your entire Value Ladder the RIGHT way...

Here's some inspiration...

If you have a physical product, but let's say you only have one SKU.

Well, your front end can be a sample of that.

In other words, you could fill in the first level of your Value Ladder with the sample.

Then, your next rung could be the full version.

Your second level can be a three pack, five pack, ten pack, monthly subscription, whatever!

Think like that.

If you have a service you can do a little teaser or taste, like an audit or a free consultation or something in the front end.

Then, that front end offer can be what prescribes your service as the solution to their problem, which is the next rung on your Value Ladder.

If you have digital business it can be a free lead magnet, like an e-book, video or something they can download, or something they can listen to, like a podcast as your front end.

Then, on the next rung of your Value Ladder, it can be a little mini-course like a challenge. Then, it can be a real full-blown course on the next rung.

Remember, you don't have to fill these in with your own products or services if you don't have them.

We'll fill them with our Dream 100™, okay?

Go ahead and fill in your Value Ladder as best you can right now: www.ValueLadderChallenge.com

Make sure to submit that form so you can have your Value Ladder delivered to your email inbox...it's going to be a serious game-changer for you.

Quick story.

I know it sounds almost "too simple", doesn't it?

The whole "find what works and doing it over, again and again", right?

Like, duh Dana, I know this.

Well, it is good in theory but it's also really good in application and if you look at some of the best companies out there, they're all doing it.

One of the best examples of this that I've seen in a long time is a place called Matt's Bar in St. Paul, Minnesota.

Some good friends of mine, Brandon and Kaelin Poulin, happen to also be Minnesota Viking's fans.

I live only about an hour from the Minnesota Viking's stadium, but they live all the way in New Mexico...so we try to get to at least one Viking's game per year together.

Last year, Brandon decided he wanted to have one of the most famous, I guess Minnesota authentic meals that you could find, called a Juicy Lucy.

In case you don't know, it's basically a burger that's stuffed with a ton of cheese. It's amazing.

The best place that has been praised by lots and lots of very prestigious food critics and influencers has been Matt's Bar.

Imagine it this way, if you've never had a Juicy Lucy before, it's basically a regular burger that's stuffed with an obnoxious amount of cheese.

...when you bite into the thing, it literally sprays out cheese lol...and there's a warning that comes with it that reads something like, "Point your burger so that when you bite into it, the hot cheese doesn't squirt all over the people sitting across from you and scorch them".

No joke.

Anyway, we decide to go to Matt's Bar and get the Juicy Lucy.

We park nearby and I remember thinking to myself, "Geeze, this is a bit of a sketchy neighborhood..."

Remember, I'm just a vulnerable white farm kid, okay...

Anyway, we round the corner and I thought to myself, "There's no way that's it".

It was.

The line out the door made it real.

We arrived about 30 minutes before they opened and there was already a line out the door.

I won't lie, it's a sketchy looking place from the outside.

As we're standing in line, Brandon noticed my uncertainty and kept repeating, "just trust me, trust me, trust me".

We finally get in and get seated.

It felt like a familiar, dingy bar.

A place you'd go for typical, deep fried food.

Nothing special.

We began looking at the menu, which had almost nothing to offer.

There's a Juicy Lucy a regular burger, and fries.

Nothing more.

Nothing less.

We all order a Juicy Lucy and fries.

Shortly after, we all make a critical mistake.

We had mistakenly thought that this was like, ya know, a restaurant and that they were able to accommodate certain requests. It started with our water glasses being wildly small, and having no ice in them.

Room temperature water in them.

Kaelin asked if they had any ice that could be put in the water.

The waitress dismissively said, "No".

No explanation, nothing.

Didn't seem to phase her, either.

And then, Dana made the next critical mistake right after she took our order...

I asked if they had gluten-free buns available, which you know, most places do now.

Even worse this time, the waitress laughed and said, "Excuse me what did you ask for, gluten-free?"

Awkward.

Several minutes later, the Juicy Lucy's showed up.

Anticipating a gosh awful mess, Brandon asks when the waitress returns with the burgers if he could get a fork.

And, for the third time, the waitress very dismissively says, "No, you can't".

Our table has now crossed the line for a third time.

It's a miracle we weren't kicked out of there...

All three of our outrageous requests were vehemently denied. We were thinking to ourselves, this is one of the most bizarre situations we've ever been in.

And, that was until we bit into our burgers...

I can speak for the group when I say it was 100% WORTH the crappy water, getting sick off the gluten bun, and making a terrible mess...because that was the best burger we've ever had.

There's a reason there's a line out the door...

There's a reason that they don't get into the fancy stuff...

Sure, ice and forks aren't that fancy...but you get the point.

They figured out what they do well.

They found that play that got them five yards or more and they just keep running it.

As boring as that is.

You know how many people go in there and probably ask for ice, forks, tator tots, whatever, every day?

How many times could they be like "Yeah, you know what? We should do that. An ice maker would make this better yup, yup, yup."

NO!

No. No. No.

That's like getting five yards every time you ran the ball and the wide receiver going up to the coach and saying, "Hey coach you know this corner's kind of been slacking, he's been going and playing the run, I could get right behind him and I could get a touchdown".

It sounds great but, nope.

We're going to do what works and we're going to do it until we're blue in the face.

Matt's Bar is aesthetically terrible, the service is poor, the menu is boring, there's no ambiance...and the overall experience outside of the food itself, isn't very good.

BUT...

What matters most?

Being "decent" at all of those?

Or, having the best dang Juicy Lucy in the world because that's ALL they focus on.

...and they do that over and over and over.

Here's what's super exciting, for you...

WHAT you need to focus on is about to be super easy once you get this darn Value Ladder filled in with your own stuff plus your Dream 100's.

It's night and day, the level of clarity you're going to have.

I'll get into more of the entire process and make it super simple to build out soon.

We'll focus on how to take cold and warm audiences that don't know us well, and get others on our Dream100™ to prescribe them to our Value Ladder.

Then, once they're in the front end, we'll focus on getting them to the next step.

That looks like them consuming the thing they've purchased/claimed, and then ascending to the next.

We keep going until our entire Value Ladder has been ascended.

Make sense?

Keep reading...the GOOOOOOODDDDD STUUUFFFFF is just beginning.

Don't stop now.

Chapter #7

"The True 'Magic' Of The Value Ladder That Gave Me A REAL Finish Line For My Business...And Why A Rat Bit My Buddy's Foot"

Is this all starting to click for you, now? There's a lot more to the Value Ladder than most think...and it's not only the difference between a real business from a wannabe...but is also the guide to creating an asset worth (potentially) millions, someday.

Can you also now see how the real businesses operate and why the great ones have been around for so long and how they can continue to be around for years to come?

It's actually pretty simple when it's just broken down like this, which took me well over a decade to figure out.

...plus a LOT of mistakes and wasted time and energy on things. If I would've had this book, and known all this from the beginning, oh man, the trajectory of my business and my life would've been a lot different, I can tell you that.

That's the not-so-good news.

Here's the good news.

You know that saying, "When was the best time to plant a tree? Fifteen years ago. When's the second-best time to plant a tree? Today."

We're going to plant our tree today. Cool?

All right, check this out.

Let's map out what your entire business should look like once you fully implement and execute a completed Value Ladder.

In case the Value Ladder concept wasn't new to you, which means you're already ahead of the game, that's totally cool. I'll still absolutely blow your mind here in a second.

So, here's the thing.

Most people talk about the old-fashioned Value Ladder in the sense having front end type offers, and then you have lower to medium offers, and then high ticket offers.

Right?

Let's take it to the next level and give you a full example of BOTH sides of the Value Ladder (front side: demand...and back side: supply)

I was actually doing a version of the full Value Ladder before I even realized it in one of my previous businesses.

Back in a previous life, as I mentioned I used to work with Amazon sellers.

I did that for years, and became one of the best in the world at exactly what my specific niche was: Amazon copywriting.

On the demand side of my Value Ladder, I was running webinars and had training programs, books, etc. that showed Amazon Sellers HOW to optimize their Amazon listings through my process of copywriting.

That was my first half of my Value Ladder (which most think is the whole thing, but it's not), which looked like this:

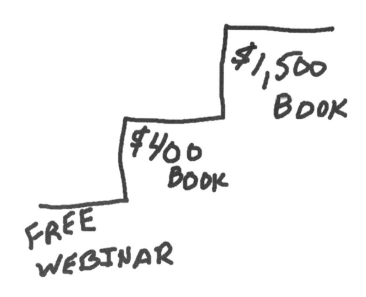

As you can see, I had my free webinar as my lead gen/front end, and then I had my first book at $400.

Then, I had a larger book which fell at the next rung, which was $1,500.

Pretty straight forward, right?

Here's what was really weird...

Imagine that a $400 or $1,5000 book lands on your doorstep as an Amazon Seller. You're excited to dig into it and optimize the crap out of your listings, right?

You start diving into the book, and start thinking, "Holy crap, this is awesome and amazing. But I've got like 150 SKUs, and for me to have to go in and make all these changes, at this point I don't even want to think about doing that."

It's amazing and will yield a ton of results and bring in a vast amount of sales, yet it's a lot of work to set it all up.

Right?

What did that cause...and why is that weird?

Here's what I thought.

I thought that everybody was just going to get my book, and then they were just going to go and do everything from the book, and then that was it.

I actually wrote the book so that I could do LESS of my actual done-for-you service. (The other side of my Value Ladder)

BUT...it had the opposite effect...

I thought this is my ticket to get out of the time-consuming, done-for-you one-on-one service...but it wasn't.

The more people that got my book, the more wanted to hire me.

I was creating a demand for my own Amazon Copywriting.

That was a huge shock, for me.

Here's what it looks like, on the full Value Ladder:

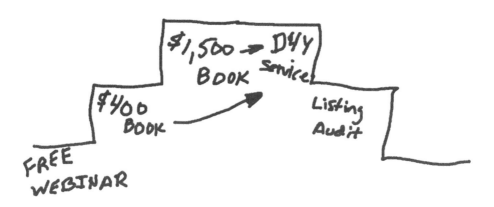

Shockingly, to me, the more folks that bought my book...the more wanted to hire me!

I had thought that they'd just read the book and go optimized their own listings. It had the opposite effect.

It caused them to want to hire someone else to do it.

Which of course caused a demand for someone to go and do that for them.

Many of the people that read those books, on the front end of my value ladder, then came over to the back side of my value ladder, which as you can see is the supply to that demand.

In other words, I controlled both the demand and supply.

^^ THAT is what a real, fail-proof business looks like.

As you can probably imagine, I had several services that would fall on the back side of my Value Ladder, which made up the supply.

On the front end of the back side of my Value Ladder, I would have a listing audit that my team would do. So on the lower rung of the back side of the Value Ladder, my team would do Amazon listing audits where we'd go through and walk through their listing and give them pointers on what was going on, what was wrong, and then we would prescribe our service, obviously, as the solution.

At that point, they could either make the changes and go on or they can ascend in to the next level of our service and have us help them with it.

That would be the next run on the back side of my Value Ladder.

In case you're wondering how much money this was cranking out...our Listing audits were $500 per listing.

Then the next rung was my service, for me to personally do an Amazon listing was $10,000 per listing.

Yeah, this wasn't cheap and explains how I made millions in the space.

Keep in mind that most sellers didn't have just one listing, they had many. So, you can do the math on that, it's pretty lucrative.

Here's the coolest part.

If you don't build this out, somebody else will cash-in.

Had I not had the back side of my Value Ladder where I was fulfilling the demand for Listing optimization, I would of just been creating a demand for someone else.

So, in other words, I would of made some other, you know, knock off copywriters or whatever, I'd just made them rich, by creating a demand for their services.

Might as well do that for myself, right?

The moral of this all?

Any "business" that doesn't have a fully built out Value Ladder, where they're controlling the entire ecosystem, as I call it, where you own the supply and demand; then you're just making someone else rich.

Plus, you're not bullet-proofing your business.

Think about the wealthiest folks on earth.

They make money on EVERYTHING they do...in ANY economy.

The wealthiest real estate moguls make ENORMOUS amounts of money in a bad economy, by scooping up property for cheap...which everybody else is losing their tail.

They're ALSO making enormous amounts of money in a good economy, by selling off their properties at a premium...which everybody else is buying like crazy.

It's no different with BOTH sides of the Value Ladder.

With my example, in a down economy (or if competition gets stiff or something changes in the niche to make the business more difficult)...there was a spike in sales on the front side of my Value Ladder.

More people were interested in DIY.

When things were cranking and everybody was doing really well...I couldn't keep up with all the people throwing money at me to take care of their listings at $10,000 a crack.

I made tremendous amounts of money, no matter what.

You need to do the same.

Here's how.

Let's flip things, for a second...

Let's say that I didn't have the books and I only had the service (i.e. only the back side of my Value Ladder). I would never had created the level of interest or gotten the level of business I did for my service, those listing audits and the one-on-one done for you, had it not been for creating the demand on the front side of the Value Ladder with my books.

So, in other words, lets eliminate the books and the training.

Here's what that looks like...

I would just be waiting around for someone else to educate Amazon sellers on why they need to get their listings optimized.

And heck, someone else would be getting paid well to do it, right?

I got paid well to create a demand...and a demand I sure created.

I was charging $400 or $1,500 dollars per copy for my books. My $400 dollar book is 97 pages, it's not even hardcover, it's softcover.

Cost me a couple dollars to print and I'm charging $400 dollars a piece.

Solid gold inside, though.

I've sold nearly 1,500 copies of that book with no advertising.

Then, I had the $1,500 dollar book, again, not even hardcover. The margins are pretty good, by the way.

Can I share an actual secret with you?

Please don't share this, okay?

This is next-level, and many of the 1%'ers wouldn't want me sharing it...

The fastest-growing businesses are the ones that truly understand their numbers.

...not just that, but that take actions based on their numbers.

For example, I won't claim to have done this perfectly...which I sure didn't...but if I would re-do the way I was running things...I would have done this:

I would have run paid traffic and done the Dream 100™ (to get others to prescribe my dream clients to me) and figured out exactly how much I was spending to acquire a book buyer customer.

Roughly, it was around $200 (I would give 50% commission to my Dream 100™ for prescribing it)...

Then, I'd figure out what percentage of my book buyers ended up buying my Listing audit or Listing Optimization service...

Let's say it was 20%.

Cool.

Now, I'd figure out how much, on average, a buyer of my Listing audit or Listing Optimization service was, over time. (aka average lifetime value)

Let's say it was $4,000 (more folks took the Listing audit for $500 than the full Listing Optimization service for $10,000).

Okay...check this out.

I know I'm spending $200 to acquire a customer for my book.

...and I know that I'm converting 20% into buyers of one of my services.

...and I know that those buyers are worth, on average, $4,000.

That means that I can spend WAY MORE than the $200 to acquire a book buyer.

I could spend closer to $750 to acquire a book buyer customer, and STILL be profitable.

Here's the math:

I spend $7,500 to acquire 10 book buyer customers (10 X $750 = $7,500)

^^ by the way, this is outrageously inflated just to show how much room there is to outspend EVERYBODY...

20% of our book buyers convert to the listing service, which means we've got 2 buyers.

A listing service buyer is worth, on average, $4,000.

That means we've landed $8,000 off of those 2 buyers on the back end.

Again, this is outrageous to consider acquiring a book buyer customer for even more than $100 or at most $200...but just to illustrate...you can see how quickly you could blow this thing up by knowing your numbers and acting on them.

Just be sure you're ready to handle the fulfillment. That's a really good but real problem you're going to have.

But anyway, you can see that all hinges and it all works together perfectly, so that's why I say there's no business out there on earth that is a complete, real, sustainable business that doesn't have a fully built out Value Ladder.

Now, again, I am going to back to what I said earlier, you do NOT need to feel like you've got to create everything right now.

You don't.

It took me years just to create just that little piece, those two sides.

...and that isn't even fully built out.

Use the Dream 100™ to fill up the missing spots.

Maybe you have them as full front of your Value Ladder, because you're the back side. Or, vice versa.

Make sense?

Here's me doing it.

I used the Dream 100™ Strategy to go out and find people that had the front side of my Value Ladder when I was just running my service (the back side).

Before I had my books, I can remember ONE relationship that changed everything...

A now good friend of mine named Dave Kettner was the piece of my business and Value Ladder that I was missing...

He had a great audience of Amazon sellers, and he did a brilliant job of creating a demand for Amazon listing optimization in his training.

Best part?

He didn't have the back side of his Value Ladder built out (the actual done-for-you part).

He wasn't a copywriter or an Amazon optimization specialist as I was, but he created a demand for it.

And so, fast-forward a few months of Dream 100™'ing him...and I hopped on an airplane to speak at his event.

I remember overhearing folks talking about this guy that was going to be keynoting.

They seemed so excited and I played along.

They mentioned the name, but I had no idea who it was.

I was 23 years old, and still in college.

I didn't tell them that, of course.

The name of the guy keynoting and speaking on the same stage as me?

Robert Kiyosaki.

Yep, that one.

That was life-changing, of course.

After that, I'd come into his Facebook group and provide value, give free copy or Amazon listing optimization lessons.

I'd hop into Dave's group and cash-in on the demand that he created and help double down on that demand for my service and for the back end of Dave's Value Ladder.

Ready for my favorite part of this arrangement?

I would fill up my schedule with $10,000 listing optimization projects, and didn't have to really do anything special because Dave already created the demand for it.

No hard selling.

No awkward pitching.

No convincing.

It's a win-win for everybody.

How often is it a win-win for everybody?

Only when done this way.

Think about any purchase on earth.

A new car, a house, right?

Unless you've got the cash, it is not a win-win, and even if you do have the cash it's still not a win-win.

You know when you buy a house on a mortgage, that is a win-lose. It may FEEL like a win for you because you're "building equity", but you know who it is an actual win for?

The bank.

If you make their minimum monthly payment for 30 years and then finally pay off your house, guess how much it ACTUALLY costed?

Not the purchase price, because the bank made a whole heck of a lot of money of off the interest on that mortgage.

So, that's a win-lose.

The only time and place that there's a true win-win in a high-ticket selling environment is when the person wanting to buy it has an extreme desire for the thing already and the person trying to sell it delivers exactly what they want.

We want a house, yes.

Do we want the interest on the loan, though? No.

It's something we have to deal with in order to get the house if you don't have the financial means to get the house without the loan, right?

See the difference?

Those Amazon sellers wanted to optimize their listings, but didn't want to do it themselves.

I plugged the hole, for them.

Win-win.

So, with that being said, that's why I get so excited about it and again think of how amazing that is to not have to create that other side of your Value Ladder right away.

I remember thinking about Dave, how smart that was because... and here's the third win.

It's a win for you as a seller, it's a win for the person as a buyer, but it's a win for the third party, the Dream 100™ Partner, because they don't have to build the thing that you did and they get PAID.

Dave didn't feed me leads and clients any time I wanted because he was a great guy.

He sure is a great guy, but you know what I mean...

I was smart, and gave him a little kickback, a commission.

Every time I landed a $10,000 Listing optimization project from somebody inside Dave's group, I would send Dave $1,500.

It was awesome.

In other words, I got to acquire a customer worth $8,500...for FREE.

I didn't have to do any advertising.

I didn't have to do any marketing campaigns, I didn't have to do anything.

I just showed up and I just collected the check.

Plus, Dave got paid a nice $1,500 for EVERY person that signed up with me (solving a problem for his students), and he didn't have to do any fulfillment.

See how awesome that is and why the Dream 100™ is the perfect plan to build out your entire Value Ladder?

BAM.

So, lets double down on this, remember that this is not going to be built in a day, just like Rome.

The only way to fast-forward and do this in months or weeks even, instead of years or decades, is by the way of the Dream 100™.

Maybe part of the front side of your Value Ladder is already built out, maybe all of it is built out, or none of it.

Or, maybe it looks like you've got part of the backside of your Value Ladder built out or maybe all of it, or maybe none of it.

Or maybe you have a little bit of both sides but there's definitely some stuff missing, right?

Well, here's the deal.

What we're going to do is plug in other people's products and services on either side of our Value Ladder, in addition to our own.

Just like I did with Dave, and he with me.

Think about this for a second.

It's kind of an uncharted thing to some people, the notion of promoting someone else's thing or having someone else promote you.

But, it happens all day, every single day.

You've even been a part of it, I guarantee it.

Think about this, there are millions of people out there doing the Dream 100™, prescribing other people's stuff or getting their stuff prescribed without even realizing it.

Once you get into the Dream 100™ Book (the next book you're going to read), and once you get in there you'll understand, you'll realize that this is the world you need to live in.

Quick example.

Let's say you're playing a sport and you injure your knee really bad.

Crap.

You go to your local doctor and say, "Gall dangit now, Doc, I'm not sure what happened but I hurt my knee".

What do they do?

They may give you an MRI or what have you.

Let's say the doc comes back and, unfortunately, informs you that you've torn a ligament in your knee.

Now that family doc that you go to when you have the flu, for check-ups, physicals, whatever; that family doc is not going to operate on your knee.

What is he going to do?

He's going to refer you to a specialist, right?

He'll get you introduced to a specialist and they are going to take care of you and your knee, from there.

Your doc even helps you schedule that appointment right now.

Bam!

That's the Dream 100™ right there, happening every single day.

That's passing your client over to somebody elses' Value Ladder.

Whether or not they realize it and are intentional about it, it's happening.

As we speak.

Here's the coolest part, there's a whole lot going on behind the scenes that you and I don't see or hear.

Those doctors are absolutely incentivized somehow (whether above or beneath the table) and choose wisely whom they refer to or prescribe.

Whether they can a get a kickback or not, legally, there is a reason they are referring that specialist and not any others.

So, when you master the ability to identify and then deploy those little pieces, like getting masses of people to prescribe you, you will be unstoppable.

Another example, if you've ever gone through the purchase of a home the traditional way with a realtor and all that, you'll notice that the best realtors are the ones that are extremely good at helping you with the entire process.

As a realtor, unfortunately some of the pieces of a home purchase are entirely out of your control.

One of them is financing.

The good realtors work closely with very good mortgage brokers.

And so what'll happen, is that realtor will Dream 100™ all the different mortgage brokers, finding and networking with the good ones.

Same with home inspectors, same with every piece to that puzzle, same with title companies, everything.

All the pieces, taken care of.

THAT is what the entire Value Ladder should consist of...all the pieces needed to get them into the home.

Pretty cool, huh?

So, it you think that for some reason this isn't going to work for you or it's going to be hard to get someone to want to refer you or just it's just uncharted territory the thought of you getting referred...you're in good hands.

Keep reading.

I understand where you're coming from and it's going to work for you.

I also know that this all sounds awesome and it's like wow, I want to do this.

It probably feels like, at least partly, the thing you've been missing.

You also know that in order for you to do it the right way and execute on this and get your Value Ladder built in just weeks or months instead of years or decades is to do the Dream 100™.

You're probably thinking "Well, I don't really know where to start" right? Or at least "I don't want to screw that up" or at least "I want to do it the right way from the beginning", right?

The old saying "measure twice cut once" yeah, that's probably the best idea with Dream 100™.

So, what I want you to do, and I'm imploring you and we're barely halfway, not even halfway through this book, right?

How much this value has this given you already?

Come on now.

If this is the first piece of content you've consumed and entered my world with, congratulations you're scratching the surface.

This is an introduction to like all the awesome other stuff.

What I need you to do right now in order to master this and actually execute and implement it the right way, is to master the Dream 100™.

There are basically two options for you, actually there's three. I'll go with the option that you should NOT do, first...

That is to go and try to figure that out on your own or think you already know what do to. Because I've seen so many people do it wrong, and I'm on the receiving end of so many people doing it wrong that it's just really, really bad.

It's SOOOOO much easier and better to just follow a system, isn't it?

Sure, you can go and you know put together a house, you can go buy the lumber and mix and pour the concrete and build your own house and it would be a lot cheaper

But how long would that take you?

And I don't know about you, but I wouldn't trust my house that I built.

You get the picture.

So that's why I'm going to implore you...in case you haven't already...and before you continue reading this book, I want you to go grab a copy of the award-winning Dream 100™ Book.

Head over to --> www.Dream100Book.com/free

If you do that right now, it'll show up hopefully by this time next week and you'll be able to dive in immediately.

There's actually even an audio version on the order confirmation page, which you can get started with IMMEDIATELY, for FREE.

So, go grab that book.

You'll see why you need it so bad when it shows up...and will have your mind blown by the time you reach page 29 (what I put on there is a little bit naughty, hope that's okay)...

Also, if you are the type of person that is like me where once you get into something good, you go ALL-IN...and immerse yourself completely...I would highly recommend also investing in the Dream 100™ Challenge, which gives you all the tools you'll need to deploy this QUICKLY and the RIGHT way.

It's like fast-forwarding and going all-in on the Dream 100™ from the start. Go ahead and say yes when you're offered the Dream 100™ Challenge, as well.

Another quick example of successfully deploying a double-sided Value Ladder...

He's an unlikely hero.

We've talked about doctors prescribing specialists and how common it is and all that.

There are certain industries that pulling this off is a bit tougher to break into. They're regulated, meaning they cannot give commissions or incentivize with financial means.

Common examples are insurance agents, financial advisors, and government employees.

So, to the unlikely hero.

I've got a member of my Dream 100™ Launch Program by the name of Galen.

Galen is in what I would consider one of the most difficult industries to succeed in.

He's a financial advisor, from a small town in Canada.

He says "eh?" and "don't ya know?", and will probably grin to hear me say that. (He's a very sarcastic and funny guy, don't worry)

Let's break this down...

First, his pool of human beings naturally smaller because he is a local business, right?

Plus, he's Canadian.

That's a natural disadvantage.

Haha, only kidding.

I love my Canadian friends, and had a roommate in college whom was from British Columbia. Ten years later, and I'm still struggling to shake off saying "eh?" after I ask somebody something...

Back to Galen.

Unlike me, my audience and pool of customers is literally infinite and worldwide.

His are local.

Second, he can't give any kind of financial incentives for people to refer or prescribe him.

I can.

Two legitimate disadvantages.

Before I get into the back story, let me make sure I lay out the point of this...

The point of the story is that if Galen can do it, you can do it.

So, Galen joined the Launch Program and quickly created his Dream 100™ list, deployed my Dream 100™ System to build and cash-in on the right relationships.

I forgot to mention something.

Galen had a third disadvantage, when he joined Launch...

(I know he wouldn't mind me saying this)

He was a boring, "me too" offer in a terribly boring niche.

Ever stood in line at 10pm on a Saturday to hear a presentation on finance?

Me neither.

After just a few weeks from joining, my team and Galen started unraveling the absolute GOLD Galen had...but didn't know it...

He slowly became an interesting guy in a boring industry.

It all started on one of the weekly coaching calls inside Launch, when Galen sort of glossed over a story...

...He casually mentioned that he was in a prison in Guatemala for like a weekend when he was traveling.

My Launch Program Coach said, "Excuse me? WHAT did you just say? You were in a prison in South America for a weekend?"

...then began to uncover that Galen ALSO...

Has a dad who's a professional Santa Clause, not a once a year mall santa, a professional Santa Clause. (Yep, I verified)

One time in, I believe it was in Belize, he got bit on the foot by a rat and thought his foot was going to get amputated.

Had another trip some place in I believe Asia, and had to be rescued by paramilitary forces.

The list goes on.

As you can imagine, our team inside the Launch Program, with the help of the rest of the members inside, helped Galen go from a boring, "me too" offer in a boring industry...

...to overnight becoming a very, very, very popular person in his local market.

He's now coined as the "Most interesting man in Financial Advising".

And it's 100% true.

Not long after, Galen started deploying more of the tools and resources to fully build his Value Ladder...which by the way he had the backside built out with his financial advising service...

...which meant he needed a front side, right?

He needed people that were creating a demand for his service.

So, he launched his Dream 100™ (with the tools and support inside the Launch Program) and he is now, just a few months later, getting his perfect client avatar prescribed by other local professionals on his Dream 100™.

Let me repeat.

Galen, who's in a regulated industry...in a small local town in Canada...is getting high-net-worth doctors (his Dream client avatar) prescribed to him, every single day.

He took the fast-forward option and built out the front side of his Value Ladder NOT by creating a bunch of stuff and spending a bunch of money and time, doing marketing campaigns.

Nope. He's brighter than that.

He just simply deployed the Dream 100™ system and has other professionals who already did all of that, creathe demand for his service, and has them their clients to him.

We even got really creative on how to incentivize them (because obviously you can't give a kickback like I could with Dave), and Galen's done a phenomenal job.

I'm super proud of how he's worked so hard and he's done such a good job of taking back control of his business by having people prescribe him by leveraging them as the front side of his Value Ladder.

It changed his life, for sure…just ask him once you get into the Launch Program, he'll tell you 😊

Let's change gears for a second…

One of the worst things that people think before jumping all in on this, is that they need to have like this amazing remarkable, unbelievable offer.

Or what they are doing isn't good enough.

Or they're not going to be able to get big name people to work with them.

They think to themselves, "why would anybody want to refer me?".

Ever thought some of these things? Especially when considering going after high-level Dream 100™ Targets?

It's okay.

I felt that same exact way, too.

Eliminate that out of your mind, right now.

Take. It. Out.

Here's the truth.

You don't need flashy.

You don't need to be famous.

You don't need to be anything special to make this work.

I've seen it over and over.

Let's go back to my good buddy Trent, who again is a local insurance agent.

As I mentioned, he's worked his tail off to get to where he is.

But, I can remember when we first started talking about it, he was having an issue getting the clients he wanted...and he didn't believe this would work for him.

I remember him saying, "Dana, why would someone want to prescribe me over anyone else? I don't think I can do this, I'm an insurance, I can't give them money, I can't even give them a gift card if I want to."

...and guess what. Trent had very legitimate concerns.

I talked him off the ledge and got him on board.

Remember, we got him selling the thing that sells the thing.

Then soon after that, one step at a time, we get him to build out the rest, so he built out the full backside of his Value Ladder with all of his other insurance products.

Now, it was time to build out the front side of his Value Ladder and get people to promote and prescribe him.

And so we did exactly that with the Dream 100™.

Less than a year later...where do you think Trent's at?

Now, he's opened up his own agency.

His dream come true.

It's been so fun to see and he's got all sorts of different businesses and schools (his Dream 100™ Targets) promoting and prescribing him.

He runs special offers to nurses and teachers; absolutely smashing the Dream 100™. Followed my lead and believed; that's the recipe.

Very proud of him.

Again, it's worked for myself...it's worked for Galen...for Trent...and so many more.

It'll work for you, trust me. Okay?

I also know this all sounds great, but so have other ideas or strategies in the past that may not have worked out, sound about right?

I get that, and it probably feels a little bit like at this point you're feeling probably at equal parts empowered and equal parts surreal, huh?

There's this weird feeling that a lot will have as they enter into my world.

You're not alone.

You may have this little messenger, inside your head, trying to tell you that this is too good to be true?

This is totally normal.

...and then the thing you're going to battle is the thought of "Well, why didn't I do this before?"

Right?

Or, "Why didn't I know about this, why does no one talk about this?"

Right?

Here's the deal...

Some do.

But, they're talking about it inside closed-door meetings.

...with only high-level folks that paid a LOT to get it.

You're in luck, because you didn't have to pay tens or hundreds of thousands for this gold.

It comes with a caveat, though.

You're going to have to take a peek in the mirror.

You're going to have to accept the fact that you may have done things wrong to this point.

You may have been misled.

I'm so sorry to have to be the one to "save you" from that...but it's here.

It's happening NOW.

Don't worry, I was doing it wrong for YEARS.

Just remember, the people that're actually good at this and get it are the ones that are silently doing it.

You look at influencers now, influencers are more full of crap than anyone.

Why?

Because they are spending all their time doing nothing but trying to get people's attention.

Paris Hilton is awesome to look at and gets tons of attention, sure.

But, I think I'd rather pick Elon Musk's (CEO, Tesla and SpaceX) or Mary Barra's (CEO, General Motors) brain when it comes to business.

They're the ones out there DOING it.

These influencers don't have much real and tangible value, it can feel like value but it's not REAL value.

That goes back to the illusion of progress versus REAL progress.

It's common sense.

The people that are actually the best in the world are also the ones that do it, every day.

Folks didn't become the best artists because they talk about it. They do it.

A lot.

The best influencers are great at being influencers, not running a business.

Think about this for a second...

When I mentioned the name Mary Barra on the last page, did you recognize it?

How often do you see her posting on social media?

Compare that to these influencers, for a second...

You get the point.

...and that's a big reason why you haven't heard of this before.

Also, I definitely earned the right to say all this, because I've put my 10,000 hours in to be able to bring this to you.

You better believe that I DO this stuff.

With that, I need you to do something for me...

I need you to agree to go all-in on this, okay?

Without that, it's pointless might as well close or exit out of this book now.

Fair?

Awesome.

That starts with you continuing to read and finishing this book.

That's step one.

Then, you need to implement what I'm telling you to do.

That's done over at --> www.ValueLadderChallenge.com

That's step two.

Then, you need to get into the Dream 100™ Book and Dream 100™ Challenge, so you can quickly and correctly deploy your Dream 100™ to fill in your ENTIRE Value Ladder.

That's step three.

By the time you get to page 29 of the Dream 100™ Book, I know you'll believe all this stuff is true.

Go do those things, and you'll thank me.

Let me leave you with an incredibly important story, that led us to cross paths...

I'll share more examples inside the Dream 100™ Book and inside the Dream 100™ Challenge, but this is one of my favorites...

I was doing the Dream 100™ well before I even knew what it was.

In fact, I can remember back when I was a 13-year-old kid, I wanted high speed internet.

I didn't have it, because we lived in the country on a farm.

Back then, all we had available was dial-up.

You can't run an online business with dial-up, right?

So, I called the phone company every week for months.

Relentlessly asking if they'd changed their mind or had made progress in digging a new cable out to us...so I could finally run my business the way I knew I needed to.

What started out as just another phone call which I was prepared to hear another "no" from...

...everything changed.

This time, the rep on the phone slipped, and gave me ONE tiny little detail that I didn't know I needed.

They said that there "just wasn't enough demand right now in my area" to justify them digging a new cable.

Just like the Value Ladder, they were the supply.

There wasn't enough of a demand.

DING DING DING!

I had it.

In order for me to get them to run a cable out to me, I had to CREATE the demand for them!

(See the parallel to what I've been talking about?)

If I could create the demand for them and have my neighbors request high speed internet, as well, it would justify them coming out and digging a line for it!

BAM!

As a 13-year-old kid, I did the Dream 100™ to complete this telephone company's Value Ladder, without even knowing it.

I sketched out a list of all the folks in my neighborhood that I could bike to.

They were my Dream 100™ Targets.

I got my list and hit the road.

I biked to their house, knocked on the door and asked them if they would want to sign up for high speed internet if it was offered.

I got 9 out 10 to say yes.

Straight assassin, at 13 years old.

In fact, the 1 out of 10 that was a "no", was actually a "yes"...a little old farmer that I ended up talking out of it because he asked me what the internet was. He still would have bought because he wanted to support me because he liked me.

Three weeks later, our neighborhood had high speed internet.

^^ THAT is the power of the Dream 100™.

Here's another...

I'm headed into my senior year of high school.

I'm playing football for my tiny school. As you can imagine, nobody ever gets recruited by any serious schools...

I wanted to, though.

What did I do?

I rocked the Value Ladder, a decade before I knew what it was.

Check this out...

Even colleges have a Value Ladder when it comes to recruiting and filling up their sports rosters.

They're the demand side.

What they need to do is find the supply (the athletes), the best ones they want to join their program.

Some high schools have more resources and do a better job of easily fulfilling the supply for these colleges, mine didn't.

Unfortunately, we didn't have the same resources or connections.

We had none, actually.

My coaches didn't even play college football, themselves.

This was totally uncharted.

You guessed it: I took it into my own hands.

Dream 100™ time.

I made a list of 40 different schools that I wanted to play at, and scratched them into a notebook.

Then, I gathered up a letter of recommendation from one of my coaches, burned 40 copies of my game film, and hand-wrote 40 different letters to each school.

I tossed all that in a padded envelope, and BAM!

I had just created a recruiting package, and mailed it out to all 40 schools.

For two weeks, I heard nothing.

I thought, "Dang, that was a great waste of time and energy."

Then, I heard the announcement over the loudspeaker, "Excuse the interruption, would Dana Derricks come to the office, please"

For me, getting called down to my principal's office...was NOT a good thing.

As I rounded the corner on the familiar path to the office, wondering what I had done this time, I spotted a man in an unfamiliar green jacket.

Our colors were royal blue and gold.

He stood out like a sore thumb.

He greeted me, saying, "Dana?".

I replied, "Yessir?".

My name's coach Thomas, I'm here to talk to you about playing with the Wildcats next season...

Dang.

It worked!!!

Pretty soon, there were multiple coaches from multiple schools showing up to recruit me.

Long story short, I ended up getting multiple offers, and signed the only athletic scholarship to this day in the history of my high school.

I got high speed internet in the middle of the country, well before that was a thing...because of the Dream 100™.

I landed a massive football scholarship, from a school I had no business getting recruited from...because of the Dream 100™.

It's not hard, just follow my system.

So, if you're digging this stuff, let's keep rolling...

Can I just give you probably the biggest nugget of all in the book right now?

Is that okay?

Literally, millions of dollar's worth of value.

Is that fair?

Ready?

All right, so what you can and will be doing by the end of this book, and as you dive into the Dream 100™ Book and Challenge, is building not just both sides of your Value Ladder, with your and other folks products and services, but ALSO creating your finish line.

In other words, you know that by mastermind and deploying your Value Ladder, you'll be a REAL company...not just a product or service.

Let's take that a step further...

You're going to build your company to either sell to the other companies you've built into your Value Ladder, or on your list of Dream 100™ Targets.

Or, you're going to build it so you acquire (purchase) other companies to plug into your Value Ladder.

See how it works?

I'll just spill the beans right now.

The ultimate end game, end goal of Dream 100™'ing is to do that.

It's like when you play Super Mario World, the ultimate goal beat the bad guy at the end and rescue Princess Peach.

That's how you win.

How do you win in business?

You end up selling your company to one of your Dream 100™ Targets.

That's it.

That's how you win in business, right there.

You're. Freaking. Welcome.

For years, I'd hear folks talk about "build your company to sell" or to "start with the end in mind" and all that, which sounded great.

But, I was left with...okay, but HOW?

Right?

I've just given you clarity on something that could (and should) be worth multiple millions to you, some day.

Send lots of Christmas cards and goat treats.

Let's end this chapter with this...

I see people all the time that don't make it.

I'm sure you've seen it too.

That's why I wrote this book.

They're not businesses, they're a product or a service.

Restaurants, construction companies, landscape companies, you name it.

Even digital and tech companies.

They kill their business.

From ONE simple mistake.

They didn't have the mindset to build their company to be able to sell it.

They didn't deploy the Dream 100™ to guide them.

...then, at the end when they are ready to get out of it and retire, they basically give it away.

Or, even worse, they let it die.

I just caught a local newspaper article that proves this...

They covered a story on a local business that was one of the first internet companies to build and manage websites.

You know what the headline read?

The headline read "Local business ends after 26 years."

You know what it SHOULD have read?

It should of read "Local business to be acquired by so and so after 26 years."

Right?

Unfortunately, the owner died...and here's what happened.

The kids quit their jobs and moved back home to step in and run it for a while, but just couldn't make it work.

They gave up.

And so the business died, after 26 years of building.

Here's the worst part.

This happens all the time.

Restaurants, same thing.

There's NO reason to not design your restaurant like this...

Figure out who your top Dream 100™ Targets are, and design in a way that they can easily acquire it.

It doesn't mean you have to sell, by the way.

You don't have to, but making the potential outcome become a seamless, easy purchase, gives you a ton of options.

I see restaurants all the time being unloaded, sold for pennies on the dollar. The investors losing their tails.

Why? Because the owner just needs to desperately get out it.

...and they unfortunately didn't do a good enough job of making it easy to sell AND having potential buyers on their radar from day one.

There should folks asking you to buy it all the time, even when it's not for sale.

Imagine this scenario, for a second...

What if you owned an American style restaurant and bar.

You STARTED with your Dream 100 List, and had potential partners or buyers on your radar from day one...

Without necessarily trying to emulate them, but putting your own flair on your restaurant...while making sure they could just walk in and take over.

That's smart business.

One of the members of my private Dream 100™ Mastermind, Steve, does this exact thing with his businesses.

He's a humble guy from a small town in southern Wisconsin.

...but he's got a THRIVING model for health clubs (he doesn't like to call them gyms, because they're not) and owns 8.

He's got them so operationally dialed in, that he has to "shoo away" potential buyers all the time.

He spends more time with his kids and NOT working than anybody I've seen, because he's taken what he's seen working with his Dream 100™ Targets, and implemented it.

He could easily hand off the keys to his clubs to a big buyer...could take a 2-month vacation without his phone or computer...or whatever he wants...and his clubs would keep running without a hitch.

^^ THAT is true success, in business.

So again, the ONLY way to do this is to:

1) Be a company and a business (fully built Value Ladder)

2) Having the right people on your radar and deploy campaigns to work with them from the beginning (Dream 100™)

That's the difference between making someone else rich, or making yourself rich and serving as many people as possible.

Think of it this way, let me make a football analogy...

The equivalent of trying to run your business without a fully built Value Ladder is like playing football without any gear on.

No helmet.

No pads.

Just banging your bare body against everybody else.

Think that'll end well?

Nope, let's like, put on a helmet and some pads...and a jersey.

Cool, now we can actually play.

Then, the equivalent of trying to do the Dream 100™ on their own is like running around the field aimlessly with no playbook or coaches.

Guessing what they should do.

Only seeing or hearing from their eyes and ears.

No guidance or help.

Totally on their own.

Think that'll work?

Nope, let's like, figure out what the score is, what down it is, how much time is left, and let somebody who does this for a living decide which of the plays that we've already practiced we should run in this situation.

When you have it all together, it works seamlessly.

See the difference?

Value Ladder and Dream 100™.

Larry Bird and Magic Johnson.

Tom Brady and Bill Belechick.

Jennifer Grey and Patrick Swayze.

Sonny and Cher.

If you try one without the one the other one is impossible.

So, that's why I'm introducing the Dream 100™ to you now, because, sure, I could get you padded up and I can get your business turning into a real business (Value Ladder)...but without the playbook, the awareness of the score and time, and the coach (Dream 100™), it doesn't really matter.

That's why you need both.

Specifically in this book, we'll get you cranking and turn you into a failproof company by getting your entire Value Ladder built out with a combination of your own products and services...plus your Dream 100™ Targets' products and services.

In the next book and resource, the Dream 100™ Book and Challenge, you'll have all the tools and resources you need identify who the right targets are for your Dream 100™ to build up the rest of your Value Ladder...plus how to get them to work with you and even eventually write you a giant check someday.

Keep reading, this is the moment you've been waiting for...

Chapter 8

"Step-By-Step How I Made As Much In A DAY As My Friends Made In A YEAR...The 2 Words That'll Make You 'Ripoff Proof'...And How To NEVER Become The 'Dreaded Newspaper Headline'..."

Oh man, we're into the good stuff now. I've given you a lot so far, but what I'm about to hand you is one of the most powerful phrases that anybody could ever use in discerning who is legit and who is not.

There's a two word phrase that will save you thousands, tens of thousands, hundreds of thousands, or even millions, over time...

If I would've figured these two words out 12 years ago when I started, I'm cringing as I write this...

...I would have personally saved well over a quarter million dollars in money that I spent, excuse me, wasted on stuff that I shouldn't have, and people I shouldn't have.

The programs that sucked, coaches that sucked, freelancers or contractors that sucked, agencies that sucked, staff (I hate to say it but it's true) and employees that sucked.

You name it, easily wasted a quarter million dollars.

Would be cool to have that sitting in an account right now. Lol

There are no mistakes, though, only lessons.

Not to mention, the money isn't the expensive part.

Here's what I mean...

The money we lose on this crap is the cheap part, actually.

The expensive part is the opportunity cost and the time stolen and wasted on it.

Yes, I've made millions of dollars personally in that time frame, and I've made tens, actually hundreds of millions dollars for clients and students over that timeframe.

However...

I easily wasted millions, or maybe tens of millions in the cost of NOT doing this correctly and NOT using these two words to prevent it.

Okay, ready?

You want them?

If you can get used to saying these two words, you'll never get ripped off again by a coach, agency, contractor, or even team member... (powerful stuff, huh?)

Prove. It.

^^ There they are.

Boom.

When somebody says something, anything, follow it with those two words.

"That's awesome, could you please prove it?" is something I say without even thinking.

When you hear someone claim something, just use two words.

"Prove it".

Gall darn it.

If I would've fricking used those two words, seven letters, I would've avoided every freaking nightmare deal I ever made...every nightmare program I joined...every nightmare person I hired...the list goes on.

Every single nightmare would have been avoided if I would have just asked for them to simply, "Prove it".

Gall darn it.

I bet you probably are thinking that a little bit, yourself?

If you just would've been like, when that agency says, "Oh, we'll do this for you. We'll run your ads and we'll make you this."

>> Prove it.

Or, "We've done this, this and this."

>> Prove it.

Or you've got that person you're looking to hire to free up some of your time and they say, "Oh yeah, like I did all this and here's this and."

>> Prove it.

"I'll be able to blah, blah, blah for you."

>> Prove it.

Gosh, Dang it.

If you weren't reading this and if I was saying this to you to your face, I'd be yelling.

I'M YELLING RIGHT NOW.

FULL-ON-HEADACHE-ENDUCING-SCREAMING.

Oh yeah?

P-R-O-V-E   I-T.

Literally screaming.

That's how important they are.

Oh, you're the best funnel builder in the world?

>> Prove it.

Oh, you've built a 7-figure agency and work with high-level clients?

>> Prove it.

Oh you're going to be the best employee I'll ever have and your last boss was crazy to let you move on?

>> Prove it.

Oh, you're a Nigerian Prince who just stumbled across an inheritance worth USD$16,601,136,111 and want to send me half?

>> Prove it.

Oh, you have the next amazing weight loss product and if I just sign up 6 of my friends I'll basically live the life of my dreams?

>> Prove it.

You get it.

Here's what will happen when you ask, however you'd like to word it, for them to "prove it"...

The really bad ones will get defensive, demand to know "why" you've requested that of them because they're "so and so and don't need to prove anything" or think that's a ridiculous request (RUN AWAY FROM THEM AND DON'T LOOK BACK)...

The bad ones will give you a lame excuse or list of reasons why they can't and try to change the subject or deflect your request (RUN AWAY FROM THEM)...

The majority will give you somewhat-related-but-mostly-unrelated "proof" and act like that's exactly what you requested or "misunderstand what you meant" after you reply that isn't what you were wanting to see (RUN AWAY FROM THEM)…

^^ I forbid you from giving any of them money.

The GREAT ones that you SHOULD work with?

They'll react with no objection, no inquiring of "why" you want that…and will simply send you more than enough proof to know they're the real deal, and what they're saying is true.

Makes sense, doesn't it?

If themselves or their thing is so good (what they're claiming)…they should have gobs and gobs of proof of that, shouldn't they?

Not just that, they should be happy and willing to share that proof with you.

They shouldn't even flinch or take a bunch of time to gather anything.

It should be all over.

Right?

Here's what I'm going to do.

I'm going to prove it.

Cool?

Calling myself out.

I discovered this back when I was coaching football.

I quickly realized that I couldn't expect for anybody on my team to do anything well, that I hadn't done myself.

To me, that's the definition of real leadership.

That's what I'm going to do for you, right now.

I'm going to prove the notion that I myself do the Value Ladder + Dream 100™.

Not just that, but I do it better than anybody.

Ready.

Here we go.

So I was out working with one of my top Dream 100™ Targets on a secret project in Idaho.

I Dream 100™'d this guy named Russell Brunson, whom I've mentioned a lot already...

He happens to be one of the most well-known human being in the world I live in of online marketing.

One of the legends.

For context, it is very, very difficult to accomplish what I have via the Dream 100™ with him...and many try and fail every day (he's told me, multiple times).

In just a few short years, I've done just about everything I could think of with him...

He's written the foreword to the Dream 100™ Book, which you will read.

I got to speak at his event, Funnel Hacking Live, in front of thousands of entrepreneurs.

I got to work on a private project with him for three days at his office, and even go to his house and meet his family.

He's come out and spoken at my event, Dream100™Con, (which is insane considering he's minute for minute the highest paid speaker in the world and only gets on stage at his own event, Tony Robbins' event, and Grant Cardone's event).

Russell's been a mentor, client, and friend for years...all because of the Dream 100™.

That's just the backstory, for context...

Here's the juicy part.

I'm sitting in his office, working on an epic copywriting project, and am struck with a crazy thought.

We're geeking out on funnels and his software called ClickFunnels, which again helps you to create sales funnels (like a Value Ladder that lives on the internet)...and something crazy happened.

Knowing that sending somebody to a sales funnel instead of a standard website is like the difference between handing a brochure to a passerby versus taking somebody on a private, guided shopping experience...I posed a question.

I'm like, "Hey Russell, have you ever done the math to find out how much more money, on average, people make by having a sales funnel as opposed to just a standard website?"

An excited look took over, and he said, "No I haven't. That's a great idea."

He turned back to his computer and messaged one of his tech to find the answer...

About five minutes later, Russell starts, literally, I kid you not screaming and clapping.

I was like, "Oh man, what did he say?"

Russell's like, "You won't believe it."

"What? What?", I was dying to find out...

Russell says, "Guess how much more money people make by having a funnel instead of just the website?"

I was like, "I don't know, like maybe like 50% more. I don't know."

I'm thinking that's pushing it, and didn't want to feel stupid.

He says, "No dude."

He's like, "We just ran this across 60,000 accounts. It's 504% more."

I was like, "WHAT!? Did you just say 500% more money by just having a funnel instead of a single website?"

"Yup", Russell shot back.

I'm like, "Dude!"

Pretty soon, Russell's office fills up with team members to see what all the commotion was about...

In minutes, his office turned into a high-fiving celebration because this was such a shocking statistic.

Cool, huh?

Here's the secret sauce.

The reason people make so much more money with a funnel as opposed to a standard website is because it's just an online representation of a miniature Value Ladder.

That STILL gets me fired up, and when I take on high-level consulting projects...that's one of the FIRST things I look at.

Don't gloss over it...if you don't have sales funnels...you need them. Get started here with a FREE trial for ClickFunnels if you haven't already --> www.ListenToDana.com

Let's zoom out for a second, okay?

We're zoomed pretty far in a funnel, but zoom way out at the business, you're going to make way more than 504% more money with a fully built-out Value Ladder...

The increase in running your business with a fully built Value Ladder versus without one is WAY more than a 504% increase.

It's going to be thousands of percentage points more money, most likely.

So, as cool as it is to have a 504% increase, that's only a fraction, if we zoom out, of the increase you're going to see by deploying your Value Ladder.

"That's cool, Dana...but...

PROVE. IT."

OOOOOOOOOO you're picking this up quick!

Yeahhhhhh buddy!

Let me get another drink of my Kool-Aid.

I did this in my copywriting business without knowing it, a few years back.

Before Value Ladders, ClickFunnels, and even the Dream 100™.

I "Jerry-rigged" an entire sales funnel through my website, which was built on Wordpress, back in the day.

I still smile, when I see it (it's still up and live, after all these years, feel free to find it!)...

I had an upsell, which I hand-coded.

Even though, at the time, I didn't know what I was doing...I was kind of offering my Value Ladder through my website.

I was building funnels, the hard way, before I knew what funnels were.

Did that with my copywriting business, revenue went crazy.

I've done that with ALL my businesses, since, for obvious reasons!

My pet supplements company, same exact thing.

I used a Value Ladder and sales funnels so I wasn't just products anymore, then poured jet fuel on it with the Dream 100™ to scale it to seven figures as a side business...which was really fun and exciting and made a huge difference and impact on pets!

In case you're wondering, I had a line of all-natural supplements that helped a lot of pets. That was really cool.

Okay, okay, let me have it...

"PROVE IT DANA!"

No problem!

...I did exactly what I've told you to do.

I created my Dream 100™ List from the beginning, and had folks that were on my radar to partner with or sell to from the beginning.

I ended up selling that business to one of my Dream 100™ Targets.

Now, I do it with my info products and my live events.

Rinse and repeat.

Value Ladder + Dream 100™.

I'll do this for the rest of my life.

One of the most cherished gifts I've ever received was from my dad.

When I graduated high school, I opened up the gift box he gave me to see what his graduation gift was.

I opened it up, not sure what to expect.

Inside was something I'll never forget...

There was a coin, and a handwritten note.

The coin I didn't recognize, but looked to be valuable.

The note read, simply, "Dana, as long as you keep this coin...you'll never be broke".

I'll admit, I didn't truly understand how meaningful that was, until years later.

Here's why I tell you that.

With what I've given you, and following my lead, you'll never be broke, either.

Value Ladder + Dream 100™ is YOUR sacred coin.

Use them, and you'll never be broke no matter what happens.

There's a reason for my success.

Keep reading.

Let me share one of those surreal moments that I personally had, so you can see this stuff is for real.

I'm sitting in college, trying to just finish and get the dang degree.

At the time, my peers, the ones that actually had jobs, were starting out and landing $30,000 per year entry level jobs.

Meanwhile, I had made $30,000 in a single day one time by adding ONE line to ONE email.

Life changing?

Yep.

For context, obviously I've done $30,000 days many times since. I've done a handful of six-figure days, too.

It never gets old.

This was my first $30,000 day and I couldn't believe it.

Want to know HOW?

...fine, fine.

I'll tell you.

But, again, it'll cost you 😊

How about you just promise to be my BEST student inside the Dream 100™ Challenge and break all the previous records (i.e. fastest ROI, biggest deal landed, etc.)?

Cool?

Let's get it.

I was starting to figure things out and started to ramp up my freelance copywriting.

I mustered up the courage to quote a whopping $10,000 for my Amazon listing optimization service...

I'll never forget it.

I was staring at my computer screen, in my apartment office.

I'd quoted $500, $2,500, and then $5,000 for the same exact service many times prior to this particular time...

...and I had a load of other projects in the pipeline and didn't "really need this one", if you know what I mean.

So, I thought to myself, "what do you have to lose?"

...and I erased the "$5,000" I had originally typed up in my quote...and replaced it with "$10,000".

I shook my head and said, "well, you just lost a $5,000 deal because you were greedy" and clicked send.

I felt sick.

Absolutely disgusted by what I had just done.

"WHY would you do that, Dana? You're smarter than that..."

I shut my computer screen and took off down the road for the gym.

That's my standard go-to when I'm feeling uneasy or tense.

I return home an hour later, drenched in sweat, and turn on the shower.

I couldn't wait, of course, so I fire up my computer...and there it is.

A reply.

"Uh oh", I thought.

I was sure my prospect would return a nasty message, explaining that there were going to go with my competitor for 10% of the price I had quoted...

Nope.

"Sounds good, how do I pay you?" was the reply.

HOLLLLLYYYYYYY CCCCRRRAAAPPPPPPPP, I thought.

Did that really just happen?

It gets better...

This was my first $10,000 client, I'd only ever had the guts to charge $5,000 prior to him.

My mind is racing, "Oh my gosh, you're getting paid twice as much to do the same amount of work."

Meanwhile, my bathtub is nearly overflowing from my belligerent excitement...

That's when it hit me.

It's just math, man.

Double your price, keep the deliverable the same.

Instantly 2x your income.

Boom.

All because I swapped out one line in my email.

I should have quit while I was ahead and scooped up the $10k that was on the table...but I didn't.

Man, looking back...I can't believe I did this.

Instead of replying with an invoice and instructions on paying, like usual, I decided to give this Value Ladder thing a whirl...

...and I upsold him.

"Hey, would you like me to take care of your email follow-ups, as well, so you can cash-in on all the cross-selling, positive reviews, and value-add on the backend?"

I upsold my other high end service, offering to bundle it with what he just purchased.

I clicked send.

"Oh crap. I just blew the deal. I shouldn't have asked that. I should just shut my mouth, taken the check, and been grateful", raced through my mind.

Again, I slammed my computer shut and ran to the shower, thinking, "You're greedy. That was stupid. You blew the deal."

Fifteen minutes later, I return to my computer.

No reply.

"Oh crap. I pissed him off. He's gone. Ruined that."

I try to distract myself and, a few minutes later, I get a reply.

He comes back, "Yep, let's do it. What kind of deal could you give me to do all that for 3 total listings?"

AHHHHHHHHHHHHHHHHHHHHHHHHHHHHHH!!!!!!!!!!!!!!!!!!!!

I was on cloud nine.

I entered into that exchange with the standard, $5,000 deal on my mind...and extracted ANOTHER $25,000...by typing two lines...which landed me as much money THAT DAY as my peers made in an entire year.

Boom.

Remember, this doesn't happen if my Value Ladder wasn't built out, and the prospect didn't come so highly recommended (Dream 100™)...

Cool, huh?

One thing that I want you to think about so that you don't die the same death that unfortunately so many businesses do, and so you're not the headline of the newspaper that your business has been closed...is this.

I want you to think about McDonald's business.

The food?

Tastes amazing.

Smells even better.

Horrible for you, obviously.

But, that's another story.

Let's look at JUST the business end of it...

Ever heard of or watched the movie on Netflix called The Founder? It's a story of Ray Kroc and the McDonald's brothers.

You should really watch it, if you haven't yet.

It's, equal parts entertaining packed with a ton of business lessons.

McDonald's gives of one of the best examples of leveraging a Value Ladder of any company.

It's no coincidence that it also is one of the largest corporations in the world.

Here's the deal.

McDonald's runs the Value Ladder at so many levels...and most of it happens behind the scenes.

They don't really make their money from the burgers and food.

I know that sounds crazy, but hang with me...

Are they profitable on the burgers and food?

Yes, of course.

However...the HUGE majority of their money is not made from food and drinks.

Well, how DO they make money?

VERY intelligently.

The food at McDonald's is actually a front end offer for them.

The REAL money comes from both the monthly leases AND equity in the real estate that those restaurants are built on.

Think about where McDonald's locations are in your city...

They've got some prime real estate, don't they?

Most are downtown, on busy corners, or on the healthiest ends of town.

And a guess what the McDonald's Franchisee has to do every single month.

Not only do they have to pay a LARGE fee just to even play the game...they have to write a check to the McDonald's corporation for the lease, too!

Every freaking month.

I'll map out their Value Ladder for you in a second, it's insane.

They have to pay for their building to sit on that lot of land just like anybody else would.

Although there's definitely money made from the hamburgers, McDonald's is really making money off of those leases...but that's not even the majority of it.

They're generating MASSIVE wealth by way of acquiring all of that real estate and getting it paid for, by the franchisees, for FREE.

It's no coincidence that they've built one of the largest real estate portfolios in the entire world.

Here's the secret: none of this happens without a Value Ladder.

I'll quickly illustrate the big picture of what McDonald's is brilliantly doing:

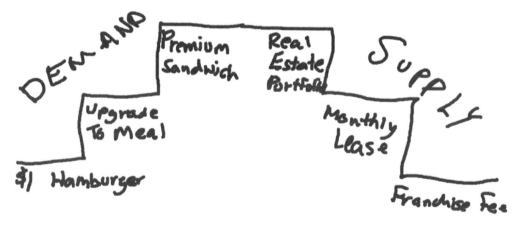

As you can see, they're killing it with the Value Ladder.

It also goes without saying, where the REAL money's being made...

In other words, here's what's happening with their Value Ladder...

On the front end (left bottom), they've got their break even or even loss leader products that they sell.

Dollar cheeseburgers, large drinks, coffee, etc.

They don't really make money on those.

Those are their front end to get you in the door.

Then, they have their upgrades...

You order a cheeseburger, what do they ask you?

"Would you like to make that a meal?"

It's math, not magic: a percentage will say yes.

Boom, their average cart value increases by asking 8 words.

Just like my cart value went from $5,000...to $30,000 in the example before.

Then, at the top of the demand side, they've got the higher ticket items, like their specialty sandwiches, their large combo meals, etc.

Those meals are where they actually generate the bulk of their food revenue.

As you can see, existing as JUST a restaurant, is creating a demand for a few things...

First, there's a large group of people out there who hate their jobs, have failed with their own business ventures, or just are investors who'd love to own a proven business model...

...we call them franchisees.

So, there's a demand from folks who say, "Hmmm, I'd like to own a McDonald's of my own".

Remember when I said that you can either be the supply for the demand you create (or vise versa)...or somebody else will get paid to?

Well, McDonald's decided to be the one to get paid...so they took their system, bundled it into a franchise package, and sold it.

In order to run a restaurant, you also need something else...

The restaurant creates a demand for a building.

With that, somebody needs to pay a lease, right?

Again, McDonald's decided to be the one to get paid...so they decided to buy the real estate and lease it to their franchisees.

In doing that, they've accumulated over $30 billion in real estate (according to Reader's Digest).

^^ Most of that paid for by their thousands of franchisees.

Not bad, huh?

McDonald's decided to make money on everything, as any good, failproof business should.

Most restaurants scrape by, struggling to make their money from their food and drinks...only to make the folks that own their real estate rich in the process.

Their biggest downfall?

They only controlled one side of their Value Ladder.

McDonald's decided to be BOTH the demand AND the supply side.

Look at the monster they've built...compared to your average family restaurant.

Huge difference.

Here's the good news...

If you're like me and enjoy a good underdog story.

The Value Ladder + Dream 100™ is the great equalizer!

Let's get tactical.

One thing that we're going to do to NEVER have that dreaded newspaper headline is this...

Remember to always simplify all your offers and, most importantly, have a clear path to and from EVERYTHING on your Value Ladder.

As you work through the Value Ladder Challenge (complete it for FREE at --> www.ValueLadderChallenge.com), you'll notice it's the ONLY way to build this out the right way...with total clarity.

Whether you only offer one thing, or you have a bunch of stuff like I do, simplifying it to fit onto ONE Value Ladder and have a clear path to everything is the secret.

Just like McDonald's keeping it very simple, and having a clear path from one step to the next.

You pull into the drive thru to order a burger...they ask if you'd like to try your specialty chicken sandwich...and then if you want to make it a meal.

Super simple and a clear path.

Then, on the other side..

A franchisee inquires about launching a McDonald's location of their own...they then sign a lease...and foot much of the bill for the real estate investment.

Super simple and a clear path.

You may have to "kill some of your babies" in order to pull this off (get rid of some of your businesses or projects), but that's okay because you're creating a machine...a REAL company right?

Then, we're going to just plug other people's stuff where there may be holes in our Value Ladder by way of the Dream 100™.

McDonald's did the same thing, they're just sixty years ahead.

From day one, they certainly didn't buy the land, the lease, and have their full Value Ladder built.

They didn't start that way.

They outsourced first.

Made the owner of the building rich, for a while.

Over time, just like McDonald's, you can certainly bring it all back in house and you can have one GIANT company that controls it all: demand and supply.

For now, we'll just focus on leveraging the assets we already have...and intelligently filling the rest with our Dream 100™ Targets.

Let me leave you with one more giant nugget...

I was out in Boise for a private mastermind at Russell Brunson's office and remember having a MAJOR breakthrough...

He was on stage explaining how he had to back off with creating new products because it was causing people to feel like they were getting pulled in 300 different directions.

If you think about it with the Value Ladder, having even 15 different products or services that you try to cross sell will just confuse people.

Ever felt like you've been drinking from a firehose before?

That's exactly how a customer feels with a Value Ladder that's all over the place.

Remember, simple.

You've probably been to a restaurant where the menu is WAY too big, right?

There's this restaurant near my office that's guilty of this.

The sign on the building says they're a Pizzeria, but they serve literally everything: pizza, pasta, steak, burgers, seafood, wraps, salads, chicken, soups, breakfast foods, everything.

I'm sure there's more I'm missing.

You get the thing in your hands and it's overwhelming.

Tri-folding, double-sided.

Holy crap.

You can also imagine the nightmare that is for not just getting customers to decide what they're ordering...but also the quality control...

Nightmare.

The systems and logistics needed to pull off all that food...

Nightmare.

The training for cooks to be able to consistently and safely cook all those different dishes...

Nightmare.

Less really is more, right?

Remember the Juicy Lucy from Matt's Bar.

Simple and clear.

So anyway, back to the mastermind...

Russell brought up a great point, that became a discussion amongst us entrepreneurs.

We all related to struggling with this desire to always create stuff, and "go go go"...

Ever been guilty of that?

Us, too.

We have this desire to create stuff because we're entrepreneurs. That's natural and NOT in our control.

BUT...there IS something we need to do with it...

...and it hit me.

We have to channel our desire to create intelligently...and we can do it through our Value Ladder!!

My heart was racing, I nervously-but-excitedly asked, "Can I go to the whiteboard quick?"

As you can imagine, stepping in front of a very respected and high-level individual (also one of my own top Dream 100™ Targets) was a bit risky...

I excused myself to the front of the room, and climbed up on the stage...bib overalls and all.

I went up there and I drew up the front side of a Value Ladder, first.

...that's all it had been, to that point.

I drew out Russell's products on the front side of his Value Ladder.

Just like this:

First, his books and podcast.

Then, his next level up is his software, ClickFunnels.

Then, his coaching program.

Then, I drew out what it would look like to create more and more courses or programs and try to shove them on his Value Ladder (which he was already saying he was needing to stop doing...) and how it pulls people in too many directions and confuses them, like this:

I erased the board and re-drew his simple, clean Value Ladder and explained, "Look at this. If you focus ALL your creative efforts into creating ONLY front end offers to get MORE people into your existing Value Ladder..."

"...that would solve all your problems."

...and I drew what I was talking about, like this:

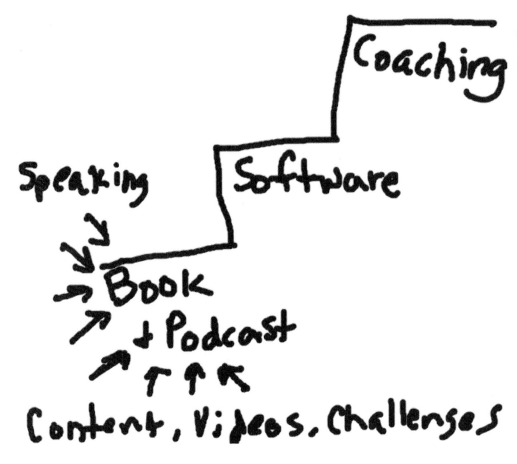

I added, "If you focus on just creating more front end stuff, like content, videos, speaking, interviews, challenges, webinars, etc...you'll pump unlimited new leads into your Value Ladder and keep it nice and simple to ascend everybody up!"

I was shaking with nervousness and excitement as I handed the marker back...not sure how they were going to react.

Russell, along with the rest of the room, was like, "Dude, that is so smart."

That was years ago.

I remember at the time thinking, "holy crap, Russell just said something that I said was smart".

That was huge validation.

I've kept a close eye on what he was doing after that...and ever since then, from everything I've seen, he has created nothing but front end offers to get more people into his Value Ladder.

Super cool and fun to watch him do that.

The little part I had in that, feels awesome.

He's obviously brilliant, but just that little tweak right there has been massive.

...and remember, it's not just Russell.

Not just me, or Trent or Galen.

It's everybody, including YOU.

I'll show my cards again.

I'm doing that right now. I'm pulling you into my Value Ladder and you're going to freaking LOVE it.

Then, you're going to go out and pull folks into YOUR Value Ladder.

Just like McDonald's does.

Now that my Value Ladder is nearly completed...all I do is channel my efforts into my podcasts, my books, my social content, my speaking engagements, and my email list.

I stick to the front end.

That's all my creative energy now and it's in my ads, my Dream 100™.

Front end.

I just get people into my simple Value Ladder then I ascend them up by blowing them away with value along the way.

That's what you'll be doing, soon.

Again, less is more.

If you're crazy like me have a desire for more, like any good entrepreneur, just channel your efforts and your creative energy into your front end offers...once your Value Ladder is built.

Dang, this chapter probably gave you more value than an entire MBA.

I feel like I should issue you an invoice?

Haha...just kidding.

But really, you can keep giving me money and getting extreme value...I don't mind 😊

If only everybody did this...that 90% wouldn't be happening.

Those newspaper headlines wouldn't be so sad.

If everybody simply mastered the Value Ladder + Dream 100™... the statistic would be the opposed.

It'd be nearly impossible to fail...not nearly impossible to succeed.

I wish I would've just had clarity on these little pieces years ago...before I created way too much stuff, and should've just dialed it back and got more people in to my existing stuff.

That's why I'm passing that wisdom to you.

and why you'll pay it forward when it's your time.

Keep reading. There's more.

Chapter #9
"An Entire Chapter Of Crap Talk."

All right...Let me just say this... This chapter is going to be all about what NOT to do. I love, LOVE getting lessons from other people's mistakes. Love it.

That's why I'm such an avid reader and why I'm so proud of you for reading this book. I'm not afraid to say it, a lot of the best lessons and the best nuggets we get are simply what not to do.

Right?

The animals that watch their friends carelessly cross the road, and turn into roadkill, got to witness some very valuable lessons.

Raising kids, I realize now, when they become old enough to go out on their own and all that, I'm not really going to tell them what to do.

That's not that effective, anyway.

I'm not going to say, "Hey, you need to go to college," or, "You need to go start a business," or, "You need to do this or that."

I hated hearing that as a teenager.

Nope.

Instead, I'm going to tell them, "Hey, don't drink and drive. Get an Uber, I'll even pay for it. Don't go out alone without a friend. Don't..."

You know what I mean?

Being smart means NOT to do XYZ, because that turned out really bad for somebody before you.

Either my own lessons that I discovered from making the mistake OR somebody else's by watching them make the mistake.

In the winter, here in Wisconsin, there can be a lot of snow.

As a farmer, it's important to keep the animals well fed and watered during the winter, as it's more stressful for them.

Like any good coach who actually DOES what I tell you to do...if you ever have the privilege of coming out to the world-famous farm...I'll prove this.

When we need to walk out to the goat pen, I'll make sure to be the last one to go.

I'll point you in the right direction, don't worry.

"Go that way", I'll say, as I point in the general direction of the snow pile near the goat's pen...

You see, I'll watch where you step as you trudge through the snow, and try to step in your footprints.

...except for where you roll your ankle or fall on your butt, because you didn't anticipate the sudden six inch drop off.

I'll just walk slightly around those spots.

Point is: I'll just learn from your mistakes and have a nice, easy trip to and from the goat pen. Much easier that way. ☺

Anyway, reflecting on your own mistakes, plus watching others...is how you accumulate wisdom.

That's all it is.

With that being said, let's crank out through some mistakes so that not only you don't make them...but you can failproof your business even MORE to never risk being in that 90%.

Cool?

For context, these are a compilation of mostly the mistakes I've made over the years (yep, I've done my share of it), but also some others.

Also, unless the mistake is seen over and over and it's something that affects a lot of people, I don't really worry about it.

So, these are just the best of the best.

The ultimate 'Do NOT kill your business, please' list...

In other words, this is me grabbing you by the back of the neck. Well, I'll be gentler. Put my arm around your shoulder, putting you in a headlock, nah, I'm just kidding.

But yeah, having arm around your shoulder and explaining to you, "Don't do this." Okay?

When building a business, specifically building out your Value Ladder + Dream 100™...here's what NOT to do...

First of all, don't try to hire this out.

Sure, you could go and find somebody that will promise you the moon, some knockoff wannabe expert, and hire them to try and build some of this for you...or help take some of it off of your plate, whatever.

The problem you're going to find is that they're NOT experts at all in what they're telling you they're an expert in...

In fact, they ARE experts, but at something else.

There are two things that the majority of those self-proclaimed "experts" are actually experts at...

Ready for it?

#1: Taking your money.

They're VERY good at that.

#2: Making excuses.

They have that MASTERED!

Quick example of this...

I went through probably the sixth Facebook ads expert before I finally said, "Yup, every single one of them is full of shit. Every single one!"

Most people would have stopped at the second one.

Shame on me.

Mind you, this one was REALLY tough for me to swallow...

Here's why...

I failed to follow the two words I suggested earlier, "Prove it.", and here's what happened...

They're like, "Yeah, everybody before me let you down so bad. That was so wrong of them to promise you so much and it's going to be so much different with me."

I foolishly believed them, and let them in.

They did a magical job of taking money and time from me, by promising me a bunch of stuff.

Then, a couple weeks in, I kind of looked at the numbers and said to myself, "Ehh, this isn't really working at all how I was promised, but let's give them the benefit of the doubt. I really like the person. It probably just needs some time to sort out."

Not long after, it gets real bad, to the point where I'm spending three times as much as I was before they came in...but was getting literally less than HALF the results I was getting before them.

So again, my costs increased by 3X and my results decreased by 50%.

Not good.

I was back in the 90% of business who are destined to FAIL...because I didn't use those two magic words... ("Prove it)

Thankfully, I recognized that and realized I had to cut it off, or address it, at least.

Remember, expertise #1: them taking your money, which they did.

Then, expertise #2: them making excuses.

Get ready for this exchange...oh boy.

I started scooping up some data and pulled out a day out of the month she had been working with us, where we had our worst sales day in over a year.

I'm like, "What happened on this day? How could it get that bad?"

Their reply?

"Oh, that's because it was Father's Day. Not because of the ads performance."

Oh. My. Goodness.

In my head, I said, "All right. We're done. We are SO done. Are you serious? Is that really what you're going to say right now? Like people don't buy stuff on Father's Day? Seriously? Oh, man. You really had to reach for that one."

Of course I didn't say that, but wanted to.

I can typically sympathize with people to an extent, but that was just too far.

Sixth person, repeating the same process.

Promise the moon > extract money from me > make lots of excuses > get fired before I go bankrupt

^^ THAT is why you need to do the heavy lifting by following somebody who's already done it (me), and leverage their proven system (mine)...NOT trust somebody who's never done it before...who skimmed through my book...and thinks they're an expert.

Hiring folks like that will get you in the 90% of businesses that fail.

Follow. My. Lead.

Needless to say, hiring an "expert" is a bad idea.

They're not experts.

If they WERE an expert, they would just do it for themselves, wouldn't they?

You won't see me available for hire, unless it's for somebody on my Dream 100™ List.

Why?

Because I DO what I preach and I'm busy DOING it for myself.

Why?

Because the ROI is much higher, that way...plus the impact I can make and the folks I can reach.

Doesn't that make sense?

Again, if that person was SO good at running Facebook ads, why wouldn't they just run their own?

Right?

Like why not just create an offer and just run your own ads if you're so good at it?

Forehead slap.

The only conclusion I can draw is this...and something I would always tell my assistant coaches back when I was coaching football when they'd try to break down and understand the unfathomable behaviors of some of our players...

...because, that would make too much sense.

Those Facebook ads experts don't run their own ads, because that would make too much sense for them to do that.

My quarterback decided to throw an interception across his body on third and long into triple coverage, giving our opponent the ball on our own 30-yard line, because it would have made too much sense for him to just throw the ball away and allow us to punt.

This guy, Donnie the funnel builder, is going to build me a million-dollar funnel, because it would make too much sense for him to build his own funnel and make his own million dollars.

Right?

WHY do you have to take money from us, and they don't do this for themselves?

Coaching hat on: because they're full of shit, that's why.

I'm sorry to say it, but I've been around for over a decade in this space, and it's true.

Needless to say, don't hire someone.

...if you go against my advice and DO hire someone, please use the magic two words...Prove it. <-- that's a catch 22, because if you use those words, you won't be able to hire anybody because they won't be able to prove it! Ha!

Anywho...

Let's move on.

Mistake #2: Trying to do this on your own.

HEY! LISTEN TO ME FOR A SECOND!

(Yes, I'm shouting)

Don't freaking DO THAT, OKAY?

(Still shouting, but adding a crescendo for maximum effect...)

It will deSTROY YOUR BUSINess, got it?

(^^ Sforzando, this time)

Stick. That. In. Your. Brain. Please.

Here's why...

I'm sitting here humbly talking about the mistakes I've made, and the money I've wasted, as I mentioned over a quarter million dollars.

That's not a little bit of money, that's an aggressive amount of money.

It's my own fault.

Mainly because for TOO long…I tried doing everything on my own.

For seven years, I thought I was "smart enough" to figure it all out.

Ugh.

Here's the less that you can cash-in on and NOT have to spend $250,000 for (or seven years)…

Lesson: Doing it alone is a no-no, because it's going to take you WAY LONGER and be WAY MORE EXPENSIVE.

Know off the top of your head how long McDonald's has been around? (Hint: I mentioned it just a few pages ago)

A long time.

Well over fifty years.

They didn't just snap their fingers and build everything they have.

No.

It won't happen by this time next week, sorry.

This isn't another shiny object.

This is real.

Real things require doing the RIGHT way.

Measure twice, cut once.

In other words, you're not going to have your full Value Ladder built out by midnight tonight, but you MIGHT have it done in just days IF you're crazy.

Some of my students are and do.

By following my guidance, you'll be able to do this in days or weeks, or at most, a few months.

When I see others do it on their own, I see them taking YEARS or even decades.

^^ Pretty rough to watch.

I humbly consider myself to be a true expert, having put my 10,000 hours in, and it's taken me five years to be where I am in my existing business. That's not counting the seven years I spent randomly trying a bunch of stuff...

If you count that, it's more like twelve years in the making.

Five years of intentionally doing the Value Ladder + Dream 100™, and I'm one of the best. (I wrote the book on it, right?)

Why would anybody want to do that, when I'm literally HANDING you everything you need...between this book, the Value Ladder Challenge, and the Dream 100™ Book + Challenge...

It's like this.

You've got this amazing auger that's going to drill for oil.

It's super rare and hardly anybody has one.

You managed to inherit it and are ready to get some oil and make a ton of money.

Which makes more sense and will get you to what you want, faster?

> Go out on your own and start digging randomly (stabbing in the dark)

> Follow my map, from someone that's already gotten tons of oil, buy my guides and tools, and then follow them to go straight to the oil

Which do you think is going to get you oil faster and more of it?

Again, don't be one of those folks that do it on their own, and our tribe sits back and thinks, "Man, it just would make too much sense to join Dana's programs, leverage his tools that he's handing to you, and fast-forward your success".

Right?

That's why I implore you, if you haven't bought the Dream 100™ book at this point, stop reading please.

There's no hope for you.

Haha, just kidding.

But really, you've heard the saying, "You can lead a horse to water but you can't make it drink"?

It's true.

That's why I also bring my goat, Billy, and let him ram that horse square in the rear...straight into the water.

Neeeiiiiighhhhhhh!!!! Splash!!!!!

Good work, Billy.

If you haven't, already, stop reading > go buy that so that you can keep reading and feel good, because the next thing is on the way, and you're going to dive into that.

Okay?

Because:

1) My goat Billy will get you, when you least expect it

2) You're not doing this on your own

No. No, no, no.

I forbid you.

I forbid you.

I forbid you.

I forbid you.

I forbid you.

I forbid you.

I forbid you.

I forbid you.

I forbid you.

I forbid you.

I forbid you.

I forbid you.

I forbid you.

I forbid you.

I forbid you.

I forbid you.

I forbid you.

I forbid you.

I forbid you.

I forbid you.

I forbid you.

I forbid you.

I forbid you.

I forbid you.

I forbid you.

I forbid you.

Alright...

One more thing.

We've got it.

Hiring an "expert"...bad idea.

Doing this alone...bad idea.

^^ Nothing you didn't already know.

This one's not so obvious.

The WORST thing you could possibly do (and the most major no-no of all is), is trying to Dream 100™ on your own, which I call "Spam 100'ing"...

Well intended people will hear about the Dream 100™ from one of my front end offers (yep, me "Proving it" again) and they're like, "Oh, I get it. I'll do this."

...then they spam people, trying to do it on their own, but say all the wrong things.

I equate it to going on a date with a supermodel, right?

You have ONE shot, if you say the wrong thing, "Bye. See you."

...and people say the wrong thing ALL THE TIME because they think it's the right thing...and it's not.

That's why I call it the "Spam 100".

By the way, I say it humbly, but it's true and I'm on the receiving end of lots of Spam 100 efforts.

My students will tell you there's a HUGE difference, because they've seen it, too.

Unfortunately, so many people that Spam 100 don't know the difference because they didn't follow my lead.

They're the horse that gets rammed into the water, by Billy.

Fortunately, that's not you!

Oh man, I have to share this quick story.

I usually don't talk too much crap, but we're friends, aren't we?

There's a guy, oh man, and by the way I don't do this to pump my chest or make the person feel bad, I'm sure they're probably going to read this, so sorry in advance.

At the end of the day, I like you better than them, anyway.

Here's why.

Going back to the theme of this chapter being what NOT to do, I could just have this guy come in and pretty much write the chapter...haha

Anyway, here's hiring a knockoff expert, getting the wrong guidance, and the blind leading the blind looks like...

This guy read my Dream 100™ Book and thought he was instantly a Dream 100™ expert.

He went and started Spam 100ing, including me.

By the way, the reason I'm writing this is because he's nothing short of being the ONLY person in the history of my business, since I've been with my wife for more than seven years, that she has said anything negative about.

In case you don't know, she's extremely shy and nonconfrontational.

One day she approached me and asked, "Who is that? Why are they so aggressive? They're ridiculous."

For her to say that was next level.

WHY did she say it?

Well, this person was Spam 100ing me, extremely aggressively.

The part that was the most bothersome was that he thought he was doing the Dream 100™.

Ugh, no.

It got to the point where he didn't understand how or what to say, or how to act, and we had to actually refund him and remove him from our groups.

It was that bad.

He was so shocked, because he thought he was like a star student. He thought he was doing all the right things.

He wasn't.

Here's the deal.

When you buy a book and suddenly think you're an expert, you're not.

Worse...

When you buy a book and you think you're an expert, and then you say you're an expert...and then take money from people as a self-proclaimed expert, but get them no results...

That is REALLY BAD.

That is NOT the Dream 100™.

In fact, that is the opposite of the Dream 100™.

That's actually how you get your Dream 100™ Targets to NOT like you, to refund you, to kick you out of their groups, and then tell your story as what NOT to do.

^^ Take the lesson. Let them walk in the snow and carve out the path, it's much easier.

Even further...

That really does a great job proving the point of hiring somebody to try and do this for you.

There are knockoffs out there that try and say they'll do the Dream 100™ for you, and it's just a joke.

Guess who offers that as a service?

Yep, our guy who failed miserably and got kicked out of my groups.

He's taking money from folks, as if he's doing so well with it, to do it for them.

I don't know if my forehead and can many more slaps, or if I can scream anymore, I'm going to start getting dizzy.

The truth is, hardly anybody on earth knows this stuff, and reading my book alone doesn't make them an expert, as you can tell, as referenced by the results of that story.

I've got so many stories.

Come to think of it, six Facebook ads experts or gurus or whatever, might actually be on the light side. I'll just call it six that came highly recommended, ending up being absolute train wrecks.

One more story...it involves $1,000 and a $20 mug.

Cool?

Here we go.

This is another example of hiring self-proclaimed experts, here's what happens.

(The moral of all these stories is to just follow my books and my programs, and you'll be good.)

This story's funny, though.

Oh man.

So again, experts at two things, taking your money, making excuses.

This guy was seriously REALLY nice, though.

Super nice guy, but horrible at what he claimed to be an expert at.

That's the tragedy of this, and why I think it happened to me so many times is, they're such nice people, a lot of them.

They're not like crap heads running a company from jail, they're nice people.

This guy was super nice and had just lost his mom, I believe. I felt really bad for him and wanted to give him a chance.

Unlike before, I asked him to "Prove it" that his mom died.

He sent me a picture of the obituary article.

(Okay, I'm just kidding. I definitely didn't ask him to prove that...or anything else. Had I done that, I wouldn't have done what I'm about to do and this story wouldn't have happened)

And again, here we go, he gives me the same, he's going to do this, this, and this for me and blah, blah, blah.

I give him money.

I send him $1,000.

He did such an expert job of extracting money from me, he even found out that my favorite college basketball team is Wichita State.

A few days after sending him money, a box showed up at my office.

Super cool, a Wichita State mug.

I was like, "Oh, this guy's awesome. I probably found somebody that's, like, legit. This is going to be an amazing experience."

Shockingly, a couple weeks go by, and nothing happens.

Well, I mean things were happening...

Just not good things.

More money going into the Facebook ads "black hole".

That reminds me...

Ya know what I appreciate about losing money at the casino?

You get to physically see the hole that your money goes down...

Anyway, more of the same.

No results, lots of excuses, and Dana pulling the plug instead of going broke.

I honestly feel like I've been ripped off so much, and have discovered so much from these fake experts...that I could write the guide on "How to run a great scam".

Oh well, another $1,000 down the drain (not including the wasted ad spend), but at least I had a coffee mug to show for it this time.

That's the most expensive coffee mug I know of.

I'm not sure about you, but I don't think $1,000 for a coffee mug is a very good investment.

Unless you want to go buy a $1,000 coffee mug, don't work with one of those self-proclaimed experts, okay?

Just follow my lead.

Keep reading, keep following.

I promise you're going down the right path.

At this point, I'm sure of two things: first, you've gotten an amazing amount of clarity and direction on what TO do...and you also got some fantastic lessons on what NOT to do.

Agreed?

You've got more than a decade worth of clarity in however many minutes it took you to get this point.

Don't slip back into the whole doing it on your own thing like I did, for way too long. Don't do that.

Let me sneak one more story in...

I'm just hopefully going to pile drive all the crap talk stories into this chapter and then be done and move on.

This one's really useful.

Again, what not to do = wisdom.

Being the "Dream 100™ guy", I sincerely enjoy Dream 100™ing.

A few years ago, I was Dream 100™ing Russell, and I created an entire book for him that I called the "Thank You, Russell" book.

I compiled over 80 people to share their story about how Russell and ClickFunnels has impacted them and put them into a book.

Side note, it was a nightmare to try and get ahold of all those people, get them to submit their story and all that, just logistically.

It was a great experience of course, and it was well worth it. It ended up being awesome and Russell really appreciated it.

That's not the part of the story with the lesson, though...

This was.

I'm going around and having my team reach out to around 100 total on the list to try to collaborate on this book, asking, "Hey we're putting together a book to surprise Russell with as a thank you for all he's done for our community, would you like to be featured inside it?"

Not everybody responded or followed through...but out of the 100+ who we reached out to...there was only ONE person that said one of the most shocking things I've heard in twelve years of business:

"No".

When I caught wind of that, I was like, "What? He said 'no' to saying thank you to Russell? What the hell is wrong with him? What did Russell do to him?"

I was so shocked.

But then, I snapped back into reality and realized that Russell hadn't done anything to him and that the person was actually the problem.

I had my team reach out and gently ask why he wasn't interested in participating in the project and, I don't remember verbatim, but the guy said something to the effect of, "Yeah, Russell didn't really help me."

WHAT!

For context, I knew this person fairly well.

This person had joined Russell's mastermind program, but didn't renew his membership after a year, then blamed Russell saying he "didn't help him".

Well, here's the truth about that...

This happened to be the same person that I personally got on a call with about a year before and listened to him explain the problems he was having.

Back then, I told him EXACTLY what he needed to do, just like I've done a thousand times before.

Well, I'll save you the gory details, but I solved his problem for him. And guess what he DIDN'T do?

He didn't take action.

He didn't do any of the things I told him to do.

People pay me thousands of dollars per hour, tens of thousands of dollars per day, and tens of thousands of dollars to join my programs and my masterminds for me to tell them what to do.

Is it possible to get an ROI if you don't do it?

No.

...and that's the point.

I tell you what to do, or my coaches tell you what to do and then give you the tools, you've got to go use it.

Common sense isn't always common.

When I read his reply, I thought to myself, "Wow. Bro, Russell didn't not help you, YOU didn't help you. You got in your own way. Like you'd probably say the same thing about me."

'Oh, Dana didn't really help me.' No shit I didn't help you because you didn't do what I told you to do."

I digress.

A personal trainer telling a person who's trying to lose weight, "Hey, you really need to lay off the carbs. And I need you to go to the gym at least three times per week."

And they're like, "Oh, yup. Yup, Sounds good."

And then they don't do it, and they're like, "Oh, yeah. That trainer didn't really help me. That was worthless."

No, bro.

YOU didn't help you.

Here's why people do that.

It's easier to NOT do anything, and then to blame someone else for them not getting the result.

You've seen that a ton, I'm sure.

Nothing you didn't know, but another good example of why I'm so proud you've gotten to this point in the book...and why I am VERY confident you're going to do extremely well.

At the end of the day, it's really simple what not to do

Don't hire knockoff experts.

Don't do this on your own.

Don't do nothing.

Right?

So, where DOES that lead you to?

Well, obviously, follow my lead.

Boom.

You already know you're in good hands, and you know this is good. We're barely over half way through this book, and you already know that this is what you've been waiting for.

BUT, if you stop now...

...this book could literally blow up, explode in your hands, or I could repossess it.

I don't know.

Is that even a thing?

I should try that, actually.

Man, what would you do if somebody showed up at your doorstep with a van with and a bunch of books in the back, and was like, "Hey, are you so and so?"

You're like, "Yeah?"

"Hey, we need that book back now."

And you're like, "What? Why?"

And they say, "Oh, Dana is repossessing it."

What would you do?

That'd be so cool.

If I were to repossess it from you, right now, you probably just got tens, hundreds of thousands, if not millions, of dollars in value.

Right?

This really is the piece you've been missing.

Isn't it?

Well, don't get ready to be done...yet.

You're on the verge of a MAJOR breakthrough.

The best is yet to come, if you can believe it...

Do NOT stop reading.

Chapter #10

"Why A Fanny Pack Showed Me How NOT To Run A Business...And The RIGHT Way To Play The Game (So It Doesn't Play You)"

Bam! We're getting there. We're cranking. Come on now! Can you feel it? That's the feeling of REAL progress. Feels good, doesn't it?

Here's the deal.

The best way for anyone to succeed in anything, anybody in the dang world, with anything they try to do, is to create a routine out of the things they need to do in order to achieve the thing they're trying to achieve.

I'll say that in a different way.

My mom was talking to me recently about something she was reading. It was really cool.

She said that people don't achieve their goals because they're focused on the goal.

They're goal-oriented, yes.

But NOT goal-focused.

Watch the difference.

"I want to lose a hundred pounds"...has them stuck thinking about losing a hundred pounds.

When they step on the scale, to see they've only lost three pounds, that's 97 less pounds than they need to lose.

^^ That's why folks get discouraged and quit.

Or, "Hey, I want to make a million dollars".

...has them focused on making a million dollars, and then they check in on the bank account to see they've only made $5,000.

That's $995,000 less than they wanted to make.

They get discouraged and quit.

My mom said something brilliant, that I want to pass along to you.

She said, "In order to actually achieve the goal, the folks that do it are NOT focused on the goal.

They're focused on the HABITS that get them there."

...And I was like, whoa, ding, ding, ding, ding, ding, ding!

Routine is an intentional habit, so we can sort of interchange them.

Creating a routine is going to be the thing that's going to get you to your goals.

Straight up.

Can we go next-level, for a second?

Here's one routine you'll adopt, once this is all up and running...

You'll follow a routine (just like I do) of creating ONLY front end offers once your Value Ladder is built out.

This is exactly what myself, Russell, and the VERY high-level folks are doing.

So, you are now high-level, if you weren't already.

Cool?

What that looks like, for me, is this...

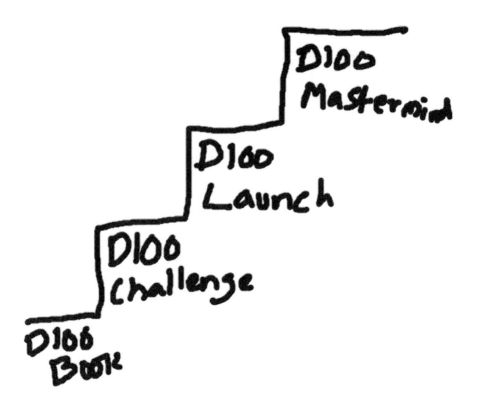

On the top, I have the private Dream 100™ Mastermind (I can't disclose much about that, yet).

Then, I've got the award-winning Dream 100™ Launch Program as my "core offer" that we ascend our best students into.

That's our "bread and butter" program that's put me on the map. It includes my Dream 100™ System, plus lots of coaching and support, and I'm very proud of it. (You need to be in there, by the way)

Now, beneath that is my Dream 100™ Challenge, which gets you ready to deploy the Dream 100™ the right way and gets you fast wins.

Then, I've got the Dream 100™ Book that lays out the foundation.

So, again drinking my Kool-Aid, all I do is create front end campaigns and products that feed my Value Ladder.

The book you're reading right now, front end that feeds it.

Other books I've written, front ends that feed it.

My Dream 100™ Podcast. That feeds it.

My email list and newsletter audience. That feeds it.

We make lots of social media posts and videos. That feeds it.

We run ads. That feeds it.

We run Dream 100™ campaigns all the time, which causes our Dream 100™ Targets to prescribe their audiences to my Value Ladder. That feeds it.

So, what you're going to do in the future, once your Value Ladder is all built out...is JUST focus on building front end offers to get people in. K?

THAT is how you blow this up.

Moreso, it'll become a routine.

Built into every week or every day, whichever you choose.

My daily routine has front end offer creation built into it.

Every single day.

Best part?

It's a BLAST!

Think of how you'll channel your creativity and be able to INTENTIONALLY do those videos...or craft those emails...or write that book.

All for a purpose, driving them into your Value Ladder, unlike before.

I have a structured hour and a half every single day that I create new stuff...and I love it!

I do exactly what I'm talking about.

That's why I'm able to crank out so much content and have authored a dozen books; because it's a routine.

Most people get the urge to write a book or create a podcast and then they just randomly do it, here and there.

No routine.

Not built into a schedule.

No consistency.

It's very difficult to achieve a goal by randomly fitting it in where you can, don't you think?

Going to the gym here and there...eating healthy once in a while...not going to really get you results.

Creating a routine where you go to the gym every Monday, Wednesday, and Saturday morning...and eating clean Monday-Friday...THAT will get you results.

See the difference?

My goal is to get as many people into my Value Ladder as possible to transform their lives, plus make a ton of money in the process.

In order for me to do that, I have to have a wide net in the front end.

That's what I do.

Soon, you'll be doing the exact same thing...and what's going to happen is you'll see an influx of endless amounts of new warm and hot leads into your world.

Here's the game with the Value Ladder.

(I told you, the best is yet to come)

Ready for this?

This is big.

The game is this...

When you get someone into the front end of your Value Ladder, they may be a customer (i.e. bought your book, scheduled a discovery call, etc.).

But, they area ALSO a lead for your next thing.

The more leads you get on your offers, specifically, the more expensive offers, the more money you're going to make.

I'll break this down for you...

It's not magic.

It's math.

Let's say you get 10 people (AKA 10 eyeballs) on your, let's say, $5,000 offer.

Whether you've got a $5,000 offer, or your Dream 100™ has it that you send people to for a commission.

Either way, we've got 10 people looking at that.

What's the maximum you could make?

Well, if 100% of them convert, that's $50,000.

$5,000 X 10 = $50,000

That'd be awesome.

But, this is better.

Let's say you have 100 people (AKA 100 eyeballs) that $5,000 offer, what's the maximum you can make?

Well, $5,00 X 100 = $500,000

Big difference, isn't it?

The game is this...

Get as many eyeballs on your offers as you possibly can.

Zero eyeballs on that $5,000 offer is...$0.

Right?

It's not about getting people in and having one transaction, no.

Just like dating.

We don't really want the one-night stands.

That's exhausting and causes us to constantly chase down new partners all the time...to have them be gone by morning. Expensive, time-consuming, and not fulfilling.

We want lots of dates, we want lots of, you know, lots of fun times, right?

THAT is how a real, tangible business operates.

Let me illustrate that with a quick story...

I remember one time, oh man, this is hilarious, but a lot of people run their business like this.

I remember I was in college and was back for the summer. I was visiting my brother where he went to college and we went to the weight room to work out.

We parked in the parking lot and, this was back when they had meters with coins you had to fill in order to legally park.

We didn't have any coins on us, so he parked his truck and headed inside the locker room to grab some change, to bring back out to fill the meter.

By the way, he doesn't drive a normal truck.

No.

This thing's a big, burly diesel truck, scary looking.

People look away and hide their children when it drives past.

Anyway, he parks the truck and then we run inside, and are gone for not even a minute.

We're walking back out with the coins to put in the meter, and that's when I see it...

...from a distance, I start making out that there's this little pipsqueak of a meter guy, you know, he's got his fanny pack and everything...

I see him printing a ticket out of his fanny pack as fast as he can.

That's when one of the most shocking things I've ever seen, happens.

You know how like when a printer's still printing, you're not supposed to rip it out? Like a receipt, you're supposed to let it finish printing before pulling it, right?

Well, he was so scared, I watched him YANK the ticket out of his fanny pack printer well before it was done printing.

He pulled that sucker from his fanny pack and slipped it under my brother's windshield as fast as he could...and then, I kid you not, this dude sprinted away.

Didn't even look.

Wrote the ticket > ran for his life.

Why?

Because he was so scared of whomever drove that truck of what they were going to do, how they were going react to getting a parking ticket.

I don't even think I laughed because I was just so shocked and was too busy processing what had just happened...

So many thoughts were racing through my head.

Like, who would do that?

What kind of person would a ticket and then run away, right?

Well, that's how a lot of people run their business.

Seriously.

90% fail for a reason.

They're so scared of the person that bought their thing not having results from it, or getting mad at them, or asking for a refund, that they don't ever go back to them to sell anything else.

It's shocking, but true.

They do the equivalent of selling something, delivering it, and then running for their life.

"Oh no, like I hope that person doesn't hate it. I hope that person isn't mad at me. I hope that person doesn't ask for their money back.", is what they say to themselves.

It's hilarious and unfortunate.

That's not how we run our business.

Again, back to the game.

The game is this.

It's not about a one-time transaction and saying "bye".

Nope.

Getting the lifetime value of a customer or client as HIGH as possible, that's the game.

Business is a game.

The game is math.

You spend X, your customer or client is worth Y, over time.

As long as Y is higher than X, you have a profitable business.

If you can keep Y significantly higher than X, you've got a healthy, and scalable (as long as you get the systems and deliverable down), real business.

That doesn't happen on these one-off transactions.

Your stuff has to be good.

It'll be good if you get into, and then stay with a routine.

My routine is something I'm used to doing now and that's why I'm able to crank out so much.

I'm not a magician, I don't crank out books because I'm some like freak that like has all this talents.

No, I just have a simple routine that I follow.

Do most people spend an hour and a half each day writing a book?

No.

That's why I have over a dozen and most people don't.

It's math.

I know you're probably thinking that you're not used to the thought of creating stuff or you're still wrapping your mind around what your stuff will look like or who you should be adding to your Value Ladder from your Dream 100™.

I promise you, all you have to do, okay, really, really, really all you have to do is, just follow my lead.

Even if you implement 1/3 of what I'm telling you to do...it's going to be a VAST improvement...

Back when I had my Amazon copywriting business, I was on the supply side of the Value Ladder.

For a long time, I had NOTHING for free or even cheap.

The cheapest thing I had was my $500 listing audit.

That was my front end.

If a lead didn't have either $500 or $10,000...I couldn't do business with them. "Sorry".

Even if you don't have a bunch of free stuff or front end style offers right now, you can always add them later.

Or...a little trick that's been massively awesome, for me...

You can transition your higher end offers into front end offers.

That's what I did, actually, with my Dream 100™ Book...

I went from selling the same exact book for $2,000 per copy (which you'll see why when it arrives)...to basically giving it away for break even.

That was hard, for sure.

But SOOOOOOO worth it!

Here's why...

I've tried in the past creating these "lead magnets", like eBooks and while I'm doing it...I'm thinking to myself like "okay, this is free and I'm not making any money from it, I should just slap it together real quick. I mean, it's free, right?"

That was also the stupidest thought I could've had.

It's actually the opposite.

Your free stuff should be so freaking good, SO good, that people are banging at your door to get your paid stuff.

That's exactly how my Dream 100™ Book, that you'll dive into next (especially when you see what I hid on page 29, by the way, which will have you smiling ear to ear when you read it), is.

When I transitioned that from $2,000 a copy to just charging S&H, I didn't do anything to it. It was the same exactly thing.

Identical book I used to charge $2,000 for.

It's so much fun because it actually never crossed my mind to make your free or cheap thing, AKA your front end thing, as good as your hundreds or thousands of dollars thing.

I correlate what they were getting based on how much they'd spent.

"If they pay 20 bucks for this, I should put 20 bucks of effort into it", was what I thought.

"Or, if they pay 20 grand for this, I should put 20 grand worth of effort", made sense to me.

Dumb.

Instead, make ALL your stuff REALLY good.

That's why my Dream 100™ Book has won awards.

That's also why people literally tag me all the time in comments of the best book they've ever read.

Again, it's not because I'm some magician.

I just made a book so good that I was able to justify selling it for $2,000, and now basically give it away.

It's the same thing with this book.

Based on the value you're getting; I could easily justify selling this book for $5,000 a copy.

I know that sounds crazy to the outside world, but you've read through 350 pages now and have gotten at LEAST that much in value, right?

After you drop this book, you'll be sucked into my world to get your hands on the GOOD stuff.

^^ Like all good mentors, I practice what I preach.

By the way, can I share another epic nugget?

I really don't like free offers.

If someone doesn't have a wallet to begin with, or won't open it up to buy something inexpensive from me, then they're probably not going to open their wallet to buy my other stuff.

To some it may sound terrible, but it's a business.

We're running a business, and the business doesn't care.

The business doesn't care because it doesn't have feelings.

That's just the way it is.

If you're running a charity, then this isn't the book for you.

The point is if you make your front end offers SO good, folks will bang at your door for the rest.

I can remember my Amazon listing audits were the BEST dang $500 somebody could spend on their Amazon busienss.

There's a reason our audits were the same price as the next most expensive person that was selling the ENTIRE service. (Remember, I charged $10,000 for that).

My competition was competing on price of their core offer...versus my front end offer.

That's like an NBA player going one-on-one against a 7 year old.

Here's what was crazy…

For the same price, my audit was better than their service!

I heard that from clients all the time whom came to me after being disappointed by my competitor.

And remember, the more people that bought my audits, the more people that had eyeballs on my next thing, my $10k listing service.

If I had charged less than $500 for my listing audit, by the way, it wouldn't have had as much impact and folks probably wouldn't have been as happy.

I know that sounds counterintuitive, but here's why…

The saying "those who pay, pay attention" is awesome…but this one is better: "those who don't pay, don't pay attention".

The less they pay, especially if they pay nothing at all, the less they value whatever they bought.

That's why I don't like free.

…and that's why I'm totally cool with my Dream 100™ Book being $20 or $40 for shipping and handling (depending on if you're in the USA or International).

Some people think I'm trying to get rich off that.

They miss it.

They're not playing the game, so the game's playing them.

I'm charging $20 or $40 because I'm filtering people.

Charging that much does a magical job of it.

You'll see in my marketing all the time to cold traffic, people bitching and moaning about the fact that my book costs $20 or $40...

Here's the game: if you can't pay $40 for a book that's going to change the way you look at business forever, let alone the same exact book that used to be sold for $2,000, you're not going to be a good lead for my other higher-ticket offers, anyway.

By NOT buying my book, they're actually doing us both a huge favor and saving a lot of time, energy, and resources.

I love it.

It's the best filter ever.

All the trolls and tight-walleted folks get trapped in it.

By the way, you certainly don't have to do it that way, but it really does help and worked the same in my Amazon business with that the Listing audit being $500.

There weren't any jokesters coming in and unloading $500 on an audit. It was people that were for real.

It works.

Do it.

I've taken so much time talking about the front end cause it's so important.

It's what feeds everything else.

Without it, you won't blow up and can't be in the 1%.

I want you to think about how valuable your front end offers are...and how amazing the experience you're giving your customers or clients is on their first visit.

Also, make sure your front end offers are massively scalable.

In other words, make sure that there's not much required to deliver what they've purchased. If there is, it'll be very slow and difficult to get folks to ascend up your Value Ladder, from your front end offer.

For example, if you have a one-on-service, do not lower the price or make that a front end offer.

My listing audits were very scalable.

I had coaches on my team that would do them for me, by recording their computer screen going through our clients' Amazon listing...and then deliver the recording to them.

We could crank LOTS of them out.

My listing optimization service, not scalable.

That's why it was so expensive, and I never outsourced it (to keep the value outrageously high).

In other words, don't lower the price on anything that's not scalable.

My Dream 100™ Book is very scalable.

Make sure that the stuff you sell is always worth more than the price you sell it for, in terms of value, build out your Value Ladder, then Dream 100™, and you will have a thriving business and defeat the 90%.

Think of it this way...

What would happen if you only charged 10% of what you're currently charging for one of your existing offers, as long as they're scalable?

...and then you set them up in a way that they naturally sold your next thing?

Here's what happens…

All of a sudden your front end offer becomes a little salesman or saleswoman, for your next thing!

Boom.

That's the game.

Play it or be played.

Every single thing should be designed in your Value Ladder, on both sides, to sell everything else.

McDonald's has this down.

They play the game well.

Make it nice, clean, easy, and have a clear path.

With that being said, when you implement this stuff, you're going to finally have an asset that other companies are going to buy or want to buy.

You'll be sitting on gold.

They can either buy you and plug your stuff into theirs…or you can buy them and plug their stuff into yours.

Explosive growth or a big fat check.

Just don't spend it all at once.

I don't want to leave ANY stones unturned, so I'll cover one last potential issue you may run into.

Another problem that people have is trying to be perfect...

To build this whole thing might seem daunting, but it's only daunting if you're either afraid of failure or are a perfectionist and get paralyzed by analysis.

Here's an example.

I am not that much smarter or that much more skilled than most people. I'm really not.

Where I'm different is I just do a lot more stuff than most.

I'll throw 10 things at the wall and if one of them sticks and works, I am thrilled.

Why?

Because I got something to work.

How do I even find out if it works, without trying?

Right?

I don't go fishing...but if I did, I'd cast a LOT of lines.

Not just one or two.

Like as many as I legally can.

Why?

I'll increase my likelihood of success.

Same thing with business.

So, get over any sort of hesitation and just launch it, k?

You have my permission.

Think of this.

Major league baseball players, who happen to be the best on planet earth at what they do, get paid millions and millions of dollars to freaking swing a bat and run around.

When the very BEST of them, the best of the best, go up the plate and swing the bat...guess how many have success.

Less than half.

Actually, it's more like 1 in 3.

The best.

They bat just over a .300 average.

What does that mean?

The other 2/3 of the time, they fail.

Isn't that crazy?

We don't need to bat a thousand with what we do.

Bat a hundred.

Bat a hundred and just bat a hundred times.

That's the game.

Play it...or it'll play you.

Here's my proving it, again.

I record my podcasts when I'm driving, on my phone.

With noise-canceling headphones.

I don't have a studio.

Remember the whole routine thing?

I'm trapped in a car for 40 minutes total, per day, driving to and from my office...so why wouldn't I monetize that time?

A studio doesn't make sense for the routine.

Make the routine work for you, not the other way around.

Also, who cares if it's not professional, studio quality sound?

A fraction of people.

Do you care?

Probably not.

The book you're reading is better than 99% of the other books you've read to this point...but you don't see a big fancy publishing stamp on it.

Nope.

You don't need all that.

It's about the content.

It's the value, not the way that value's delivered.

Make sense?

Would you care if this book showed up on a jet or on the back of a goat?

I mean, a goat delivering it would be awesome.

But not as much as it showing up and delivering value.

Right?

My Dream 100™ Podcast listeners helped prove this.

When I record my podcast, it's not uncommon for me to also be feeding my goats before I head out to the office.

I don't care.

Odd background noises, grunting, goats...that stuff doesn't matter.

So this particular morning, I'm feeding my goats while in a deep dive...and BAM!

As I'm exiting their goat pen, I literally fall down on my face, mid-recording.

Yes, I fell down and didn't stop recording.

The best part is?

My audience LOVED it.

They thought it was hilarious. Seriously.

So, if I can fall down feeding goats while recording a podcast (which turned out to be one of my better episodes), you can launch and sell your thing.

You don't need bells and whistles.

You don't need any crazy anything.

Just get it done.

Value Ladder + Dream 100™

Just get it done.

I'll leave you with this story.

You might be like this and that's okay.

For years, I just worked where I traded my time for money and I had nothing to sell, like no scalable anything.

I basically just sold my time.

Unfortunately, that's how a lot of people work and that's how they think the world is.

You know better.

The game is playing them.

Unlike before, now I make money while I sleep, while I go to the bathroom, while I work, while I drive, while I eat, while I do everything.

HOW?

I have fully built out Value Ladder.

Everything works perfectly, like a well-oiled slide, to get people in and headed where I need them to go.

It was awesome and empowering to clean my business up and get clear and focused on that.

The next challenge is to finish setting myself up for potential buy out or acquisition.

Whether that's me buying someone else or them buying me.

That's the next evolution of business.

That's where you already know the Dream 100™ comes in.

Your Value Ladder is like the foundation.

Then, the Dream 100™ is like the building you're constructing.

You're getting the foundation down right now.

Soon, we'll start constructing the building.

Then, at some point, you're either going to buy someone else's building and take over another one...or you'll sell your building to someone else.

THAT is where the real money's made.

Play the game.

I want my newspaper headline to read: "Local entrepreneur has record acquisition"

Not: "Local business shuts it's doors after 46 years"

Which do YOU want?

Keep reading.

The game's not almost over...it's almost starting.

Chapter #11
"The Single Biggest Business Secret You'll Discover This Year."

We are CRANKING. How about a quick dirty little secret, from my family to yours...

To me, this is what makes business super fun. This is also how you play chess 6 moves ahead of your opponent.

You don't have to make money on the front end.

I know, you've gathered that...by now.

Let's deep dive, there's more gold to get.

This means you don't need to acquire customers profitably when you have a fully built out Value Ladder.

90% of businesses don't know this or operate that way. They live and die by the margins of whatever they sell.

That's also why they fail.

You certainly CAN and SHOULD make money on your front end, of course.

But, you don't have to.

For example, my Dream 100™ Book doesn't make me any money.

After affiliate commission or ad spend, plus printing and fulfillment costs, I basically break even.

I'm good with it.

Why? Because I'm acquiring new leads and customers for free.

That's what YOU'RE going to do, too.

That's what your front end is designed to do.

Back when I was doing my freelance copywriting in the Amazon seller space, my listing audit was profitable...but didn't HAVE to be.

I charged $500 for each I sold, I sent $250 commission to my Dream 100™ Partner that prescribed me, and paid my coaches $50 to complete one.

I pocket $200, for free.

Then, because of math and not magic, a percentage of them would also buy my $10,000 listing service.

My competitor?

Lived and died by her $500 listing service.

If I wanted to...

I could have slashed the price of my Listing audit to, say, $200. Still had room to give $100 commission to my affiliate, $50 to my coach, and $50 in my pocket.

I would have gobbled up just about all the market, by doing that (less than half the price for something even more valuable than my competitor), and would have taken out almost everybody.

They were living and dying by that $500 margin...and wouldn't have been able to compete on my lower price, because they were competing against my front end offer with their core offer.

Even better?

I would have acquired even MORE Listing audit clients...which means MORE eyeballs on my $10k Listing service.

If I didn't accidentally blow it up and things got so out of control...I would have ran the exact play I just explained.

But, I had to pivot.

When I figured out the missing half of my Value Ladder, I knew I had to start controlling the demand side...and fill in what my Dream 100™ Targets had been doing...

I came out with a guide that showed Amazon sellers how to optimize their listings, which was a $400 on the demand side on my Value Ladder.

That book gave my customers tremendous value, and also sold the next book which was $1,500.

Because of math, a percentage of buyers came back and bought the next book.

In theory, I could spend up to $400 (whether affiliate commission or ad spend) to acquire a buyer of that book, because about 25% of people that bought the $400 book, ended up buying the $1,500 book.

That was with very minimal effort, by the way.

My $400 book was my "thing that sold the thing".

I could spend up to $400 and still remain profitable.

I didn't need to do nor did I do that, obviously. But you get what I'm saying, right?

When you have high-ticket offers (or send your people to your Dream 100™'s high-ticket offers), your front end becomes a machine that feeds you.

Something you'll be able to do right now to cash-in on my little secret is this...

I've talked about this before, but it's worth doubling down on.

Turn your customers into leads for another thing.

HOW?

Figure out what problems they have, next.

Don't look at them as a customer, anymore.

Look at them as a lead.

What's the next logical thing. Part of the magic sauce is the next thing doesn't have to be yours necessarily, right?

Tangible example.

Back to the Amazon business.

My demand side of my Value Ladder had my $400 and $1,5000 books, and that was it.

I didn't have coaching.

I didn't have masterminds.

I didn't have high-ticket on the demand side.

Again, on the supply side I had the $500 Listing audits, the $10,000 Listing service, and a $30,000+ custom one-on-one done-for-you.

What did I do?

I plugged those holes with my Dream 100™.

When people came to me and asked for coaching on their Amazon business, I said, "ah, I'm not really an Amazon selling expert. I'm just the best in the world at taking your listing and then optimizing it for both traffic and conversions. That's my wheelhouse."

As I mentioned, I DID go on to build a seven-figure Amazon business of my own, eventually.

BUT...

As I mentioned earlier, letting those leads go down the road was wasteful.

What did I do, instead?

I prescribed them to my buddy, from before, Dave Kettner.

I would send people looking for coaching back over to him.

He was the supply.

It was really cool.

I simply turned them back into a lead.

Then once they became a lead, I had a place for them to go and a clear, easy path for them to get there (Dave set me up a private landing page to point my folks to).

People seem to get hung up on this or they might want to quit or whatever.

What happens here is people think in theory it makes sense, but then they don't apply it.

Here's what will happen to them.

Like I said in previous chapters, they'll stay right where they are.

The game will play them.

I see it too much. It sucks.

It sucks watching someone not take your advice and not do what you tell them to.

I had the other day, a guy on the fence about something and I just was like, you know, you're on the fence.

Sorry, but we can't work together.

I don't do that.

I'm fortunate enough to have earned the right to NOT have to work with people that aren't all-in from the get go.

I'm not going to drag, push, pull somebody into any of my programs.

It'd cost more time and energy and probably wouldn't be a good fit, anyway.

I'm not going to say there's no hope for him, but he is on a terrible path. He is on a painful long path and it just sucks. But that's what happens when people don't implement.

One of the coolest sayings that I've seen in a long time came from a low point in my life...

Back in college, I had a pretty serious relationship and the gal ended up cheating on me with the local tattoo artist in town. So that was pretty sweet.

I was devastated, totally heartbroken, and all messed up for a while.

I remember talking to a therapist or whatever could have paid him all the money to just say this and that would have been probably the amount of value I needed...

He said, "yeah, people sometimes unfortunately think that the grass is going to be greener on the other side. And the truth is that it's just the grass is greener where you water it."

And I was just like, "Dude, you just...mic drop".

Maybe you've heard that one before?

It's the truth.

So the guy that I didn't accept into our program because he wasn't all-in and I wasn't sure, will know soon that the grass would have been greener because he could have watered it.

He can go search for something else.

Don't worry, I'm way guilty of this.

$250,000 wasted.

Here's the truth...

This is your grass.

You now see your grass for the first time.

...and you also see that your grass is not totally green, yet.

Even better, you see what green grass looks like.

McDonald's has green grass.

Trent has green grass.

Galen has green grass.

I have green grass.

The folks that inhale my Dream 100™ Book and join my Challenge, have green grass.

Everybody else promises "green grass, green grass, green grass"...but they don't even know this stuff.

They take our money, then make excuses and our grass never gets greener.

Right?

But we keep hearing the same thing over and over.

"Oh, your grass will be green over here, you need this", and we'd go chase these things and none of it actually works.

Right?

Like if we could just be honest, almost none of the crap we've invested in has opened our eyes the way this has.

Am I right?

We've now, for the first time, identified where the hell your grass is...and what green grass actually looks like.

My grass is right here and I'm not jumping that fence anymore. I don't need anything else.

Here's what very savvy entrepreneurs are repeating: "I'm going all-in on Value Ladder + Dream 100™ and Dana Derricks. Sorry, bye. I'm off the market. I'm team Dana now".

Let's water your lawn.

This book has showed you where your lawn is because every other person before me drug you over to their yard and said that you can have green grass if you head over there.

You got there, there was no green grass and they made up excuses for that. And then you left and were on to the next thing.

No more.

I've already tried everything.

There have only ever been two things that have ever actually consistently worked for me and actually helped my business.

You know them.

Since you're all-in on those two things, you're going to wake up soon with a failproof business.

Having your Value Ladder fully built makes you have something for everybody.

Since you're reading this, you've already entered my Dream 100™ Value Ladder (the greatest decision you've made this year, by the way).

You're going to see.

Maybe you're ready to go all-in on the Dream 100™ and you want to apply for the Launch Program?

It's math.

A percentage will.

Maybe you want to start with just the Dream 100™ Book because you're a tight-britched fella.

You're a tight-britched bloke.

I don't know.

I've been calling people blokes lately because the folks I say it to don't what that is, but I don't really either.

I have some members of my Launch Program that are from the United Kingdom, and they keep calling me it.

But, they say it in a nice way, so I don't think it's an insult? They said, "You're an inspirational bloke," or something like that.

Anyway, you'll probably tear through the Dream 100™ Book and Challenge, go and get some crazy value...

...and unlock the sequel, the Dream 100™ Book: Reloaded!

You'll then dive into the longest book marketing in history, and then implement.

You'll get more value, and make more money.

Then, you'll use that money to keep climbing my Value Ladder.

It's literally like a broken slot machine that you always win.

You put $20 in, or whatever you paid for this book, you've gotten THOUSANDS of dollars of value out.

What happens when you put $500 in?

Are you going to get $5,000 out?

What happens when you put $10,000 in?

Are you going to get $100,000 out?

If I had to choose ONE thing to throw money at...it's this stuff.

The grass will be very, very green.

I'll leave you with a quick story.

Whoever originally said, "you are the product of the like five closest people to you", they deserve a giant high-five.

It's so true.

It's super important and I'll deep dive a little more on this when you get into the Dream 100™ Book...but let me give you a little teaser.

When you double down on the right people, it's inevitable for you to wake up someday soon with the business you've always wanted...withOUT the pressure and noise of the crap that you're dealing with.

It's inevitable.

There's a reason I have more social proof than most of the other gurus combined.

It's logic.

There's a reason I get tagged every single day all day with people saying, "Dana! I can't believe this is happening!!! "

And I'm like, "Yeah, I can believe it cause I've seen it before".

This changed my life.

...and there's a reason that I'm reaching you through this book right now.

There I sat.

In the basement of my church on a Saturday morning, with around 30 other men.

I'm in the middle of a men's ministry class...and I have one of the biggest discoveries of my life.

My pastor was explaining the topic of surrounding yourself with the right people.

Something he said stuck with me, and I'll remember it for the rest of my life...

I love sharing this story because It's so true and so important.

He asks us, "How many of you really want to, you know, make a dent in the world and the impact a lot of people?"

I said to myself, "Ummm hello! You're speaking to me".

I never really thought about it the way that he does until he did this demonstration...

He said, "all right, here's what I need you to think about, look at that brick wall right there," as he pointed at the brick wall.

He explained, "all right, you see all those bricks?"

We're like, "Yep."

He's like, "You're all wanting to impact all those bricks? Right? That's all the people you want to impact."

I'm like, "Yep."

"All right", he said, "this is what people do wrong. They try to impact every single brick, brick by brick, one at a time."

And I'm like, "yeah? "

He's like, "no. Here's what you need to do. See that brick in the middle?", and he lazered in on one brick in the very middle of the wall. "If you look at that, that's you. Okay? Now you see how there's five bricks connecting to it?"

He started pointing at the five bricks that are connected to it directly to it. "So there's five bricks that each connect to that brick, to you", he explained.

He's like, "you need to go all-in on those five bricks. And see how those five bricks connect to five bricks? And then those five bricks connect to five bricks?" as he started waving his hand and covered the entire wall..

"You see how all of a sudden you've connected an entire wall by just doubling down on those five people?", he asked.

And I was like, "Oh man, you just dropped the funk bomb on us all today, pastor Mike!!!!"

It was the coolest thing because ever since that moment, I have painfully cut back on a lot of the relationships that were weighing me down, even the good relationships, because I wasn't able to impact them enough.

You may have to cut out the high school friend who's actually not much of a friend, because they get jealous of you.

Or, you may have to cut out the family member that's super toxic and feels like they have the entitlement but feels like they can get away with it because they were born out of a related you know where.

I literally deleted phone apps, contacts, everything I had to.

Get away from it.

Stick to five.

I physically can't keep up with all the people that message me every day.

Even when I began Dream 100™'ing, I was guilty of this.

I tried to Dream 100™ everybody, one by one, and that turned out to be stupid.

I was just doing a crappy job with more people. I should have done a brilliant job with fewer.

Right?

Then, I DID start doing that.

Less is more.

Everything changed.

With that being said, I sincerely hope to earn the right to be one of your five that you know impacts you the most.

And if that means you double down and you shut everything else off in your business, you fire your existing coach and jump in with me, so be it.

My team and I are up for the challenge and I'm more than willing to step up and help.

That's what I've designed for you.

I've designed all that to help you in every piece of your business and to actually get the results you're wanting so that you can solve the problems that have been lingering.

You know...maybe you're working 12 or 16-hour days and you don't want to...

Or maybe you have clients that are sucking the life out of you....

Whatever you're dealing with, you don't have to deal with anymore.

Maybe you have stress of money every month and it feels like you can never get ahead.

I mean it when I say you don't have to deal with that anymore.

Maybe you have people that don't support you and it's very difficult for you to get the job done.

You don't have to do that anymore.

I'm telling you, just follow my lead.

Let me be one of the five and Bam!

You're going to be my 70000th success story.

Okay?

Pretty much inevitable.

You do your part.

Follow what I'm telling you and the rest of the history.

Finish out this book strong.

You're almost there.

Feels pretty good, huh?

Chapter #12
"The 5 Dominoes To Topple Over For Success NOW!"

All right. Let's get into some dominoes and leave you with some dang tangible progress, cool? Let's go over the five biggest dominoes that you can push over to get you closer to your goals, right now.

Actually, I'm going to do six, maybe.

I'll even give you a bonus one.

Domino #1: Get clear on WHAT it is you have to offer.

If you haven't already, head over to --> www.ValueLadderChallenge.com and go through it.

The first step is to lay everything on the table.

Ever played the board game, Scrabble?

When you set the game up, you have a bag full of random, mixed up letters.

All the letters are in a bag and you can't see any of them.

You can't spell anything or play the game without seeing the letters. So, what do you have to do?

The very first thing you do before you start playing, you pull all the pieces out and you lay them on the table.

Then, you turn them upright, so you can see all the letters.

That's what we're doing first, in the Value Ladder Challenge.

I did this, myself, on a whiteboard.

Just lay out all the crap that you sell and have created.

Everything, even the old stuff.

I filled a whiteboard, by the way, so don't feel bad.

Domino #2: Now we have to figure out how we can repurpose that stuff, especially if some of it isn't very congruent, so that they all fit into ONE Value Ladder

Now, we simply figure out what you can repurpose and then shove into one Value Ladder.

If stuff doesn't make sense, it might have to go.

You might not be able to use it. Might have to kill the baby. Sorry. It's a good, bad thing.

Again, figure out what can fit where and it's actually really easy to do, too, because you just adjust the price and move things around.

Remember what I said before?

Maybe you have a program you've been selling for $1,000 or $2,000.

What would happen if you sold it for $50?

Everybody would go crazy and say, "This is the best $50 I've ever spent," right?

Like my Dream 100™ Book, remember?

It sat at $2,000, midway up my Value Ladder.

Didn't make sense for it to sit there.

That's why when I wrote all this out on my whiteboard, I did exactly what I'm telling you to do.

I pulled the book back down and turned it into a front end offer.

You're going to do the same thing, if you need to repurpose something.

Again, if there are products or services that don't fit, don't stretch it so much. It doesn't fit, it doesn't fit. Revisit it.

Keep moving.

We're not going to have a Value Ladder that's all over the place. That's bad.

Also, on the other hand, if you don't have a bunch of stuff, don't feel bad. That's okay.

We'll fill it with our Dream 100™.

Domino #3: Take all that stuff that you have and put it on your Value Ladder.

You don't have to fill your entire Value Ladder, of course, specifically both sides. Just fill it for what you have.

If you only have one thing, put one thing on there. That's it.

You don't need to force feed your Value Ladder.

Do it wisely.

Do it right.

Measure twice, cut once.

Put your best stuff on there.

Domino #4: Figure out which pieces of your entire Value Ladder (supply and demand, front and back) you're going to need to fill with your Dream 100™ Targets

Mark those spots as "Dream 100™", and you'll fill those later (with the guidance of my Dream 100™ Book & Challenge, of course).

Domino #5: (If you haven't done this, there's something wrong and the repo man is going to be knocking.) Get the Dream 100™ Book

Head over to --> www.Dream100Book.com/free

Dive in. Inhale it.

That'll explain WHO your Dream 100™ will be and WHAT promotions to run with them...

Then, head to --> www.Dream100Challenge.com

That'll give you the tools you need to know WHERE to find them, WHAT to say to them, and HOW to get them to work with you...so you can build the rest of your Value Ladder.

Trust me, you don't want to skip this.

You know how expensive it is to skip this?

If I wouldn't have had Dave Kettner back in my Amazon copywriting days, I wouldn't have been able to charge NEAR $10k per listing.

I would have been biting, scratching, and clawing for the $500 clients, just like my competitor.

Struggling.

It's that critical.

If it wasn't for him, I literally would not have been sitting in the back of my college marketing class my senior year, my final semester in college, 23 years old making $336,000.

For context, that's more than the president of the university.

That doesn't happen without Dave.

THAT is the power of the Dream 100™.

Take that seriously.

Get the book and challenge, the price is stupid.

You're going to print money as you go through the challenge and then you're going to unlock the largest, longest marketing book in history...and print even more money.

Page 79.

Just remember, page 79.

All right. We're clear.

Good.

When you knock those five dominos over, what's going to happen is you're going to build your business sustainably the right way and have extreme clarity on what the heck you're building.

That's important, right? It's like blueprints.

This is interesting.

It's going to be some ripple effect, too.

I actually had one of the biggest surprises in my career by doubling down on Value Ladder + Dream 100™.

Ready for it?

I found my purpose again in what I was doing...and even fell in love with my business again.

The same will happen to you, soon.

I promise.

Galen, one of my Dream 100™ Launch Program members who I talked about earlier, did a Facebook live with me because he's been such a good student and ambassador of the Dream 100™ done right.

On the live he said something that really made me stop and just be like, wow.

Wow.

This matters.

This really matters.

Here's a sneak peek inside the Launch Program...

One of the first parts is identifying and then leveraging your superpower.

That's one of the best ways to do the Dream 100™ correctly. That's what I did through my copywriting.

Galen told me that he credits identifying his superpower to feeling like he found his purpose.

That was just a couple months ago that he did that, he went through that transformation and it really made me stop and think, wow this stuff is bigger than me.

To think that there are people out there that are running their business just going through the motions is pretty...it's the reason I get up and do this. It's the reason I'm writing this to you.

It's true, you really don't know what you don't know.

I'm telling you, the ripple effect here is that you're going to find significance and purpose and fall in love with what you do again.

That's exactly what happened for me.

I was broke.

It got me out.

Then, I was miserably rich.

It got me out.

No matter what situation I found myself in, Value Ladder + Dream 100™ got me out.

It'll get you out.

Every day, my goal is to inspire as many entrepreneurs as I can to use the Dream 100™.

That's exactly what I'm doing right now and it's my perfect day. It doesn't feel like work. It truly doesn't.

There are a lot of times where I will stretch that hour and a half of my routine because I'm having so much enjoyment by getting another message out to someone that needs it.

I hope that that's you.

You're almost there, don't stop.

Let's take this home.

Chapter #13
"There's A Circus Going On"

hate that I have to write this chapter. But I do, it's critically important. Here's why...

The majority of people out there that don't get results in what they're doing, they're actually sabotaging themselves and they don't even know it.

Or, they're being sabotaged by an external person.

Or, both.

Here's a glaring example.

Let's say that there's a mom and wife whom decides that she wants to get healthy and lose a bunch of weight.

First of all, she can sabotage herself by being undisciplined, by having a lack of knowledge in thinking that what she's doing is helping but it's really not, by cheating on her routine, or even by not doing anything that she's supposed to do.

Lots of ways she can self-sabotage.

Being sabotaged by themselves is easy to see, but what's not so obvious is how people are sabotaged by others.

Here's how the mom and wife might get sabotaged by an external person...

Her husband or her kids might not understand or respect her new decisions. They might ask her to continue to go to the same restaurants, not give her the hour a day she needs to get to the gym, or even think that what she's doing is crazy and not support her.

Those are just a few of the many ways that she can get sabotaged, by others.

Most likely, there's a combination of self-sabotaging and/or external sabotaging going on and it's happening to all of us in our businesses.

One of the worst offenses of self-sabotaging that I come across is the notion that somebody will read my book and then think that they "get it" and then go run off and they go do it wrong.

It's both sad and frustrating to watch.

I already gave you that example of the guy that did that and we had to shut him down and kick him out and refund him. That is not, not, not, not at all how this works, my friend. I know that's not you and we both obviously can agree on that.

The external sabotaging, which you'll see more of inside the Dream 100™ Challenge, is the people out there that all they care about is extracting money from you.

I brought this up before, but I'm about to show you how to not just play the game...but WIN the game...so you never lose.

I said it before, they make you feel like you're making progress and that's what keeps you coming back...but in reality you're not.

^^ As you know, that's the illusion of progress.

Tangible progress, on the other hand, looks like THIS...

"Oh man, I've just closed a deal worth a LOT last week", or, "I just got this result from my client or my customer and this is what happened", or, "my bank account has this in it now and it had that in it before."

That's tangible progress.

You can calculate it with a calculator.

Conversely, the "experts" want us to instead FEEL like we're getting somewhere.

It's a whole heck of a lot easier to feel progress than to actually achieve it.

Plus, if we feel like we're getting somewhere, then they become the hero and appear to be helping us.

But here's the reality, the sad reality is this.

Those fake experts are NOT giving us real progress by having us watch their videos or listen to this or constantly consume that...

Unless they're explicitly telling us exactly what to do or not to do, like this book, plus giving us the tools to do it, like in EVERYTHING you find from me, it's all an illusion.

I'll prove it

My Dream 100™ Challenge is literally two and a half hours of nothing but, "Go do this, here's the tool, go use it."

People get out of it with SO MUCH clarity, it's crazy. Why?

Because I don't just have them watch videos and say, "oh, that sounds like a good idea."

I haven't had you do that, even in this book.

You probably have done more from this book than probably most of the other books you've ever read, combined.

How do I know?

Because I know that the game is not just keeping your eyeballs on me as much as I can to then extract as much money from you as possible, then head over to the next person.

No.

I have, from day one, always realized and recognized the value of and respected the thought of a long-term relationship.

Selfishly, I can make SO MUCH more money from you (or anyone else) by helping you make more money yourself.

You put a dollar in with me, and I get you a thousand back? What are you going to do next? Then, you put a thousand in and I help you get ten thousand back?

That's the game.

Back in my Amazon copywriting days, I understood that the second project was always worth more, then the third and the fifth and the tenth were where the REAL money was made.

That was the game.

The majority of my businesses always repeat business.

Why? Because I over-deliver, always. I always give way more value than the price that I'm paid. And that's what you're about to do.

Football coaching hat on for a second.

I need you to shut off the external saboteurs.

Even if they're highly respected.

Even if it doesn't seem like they could ever do that to you.

Even if it's hard.

A lot of times, they have good stuff to say, but at the end of the day it doesn't move the needle.

It needs to, or you're just wasting time.

Your business doesn't have feelings, your business doesn't need to be entertained, your business doesn't need to do anything except serve you and make you money and then serve the people that you work with.

That's it. The business doesn't care.

If you want entertainment go watch a movie, go to a play, go watch a baseball game. That's what that stuff's for.

If you want to actually turn your business into what you know it needs to be, shut them off, shut those people off.

I know you're probably thinking right now, "Oh man, is that really what they're doing?"

Yes.

They are.

Yes, I've sat in meetings, private meetings where they have openly said that that's what they're doing.

I won't win a popularity contest for telling you that, either.

It really is terrible.

It's manipulation, and I'm sorry to be the bearer of bad news.

If they're not saying, "Stop, go do this" or, "stop, take this tool, go use it"...they're not actually helping you.

They're not helping us, we're just part of the circus.

It's a circus and they're the clown.

THAT is a real saboteur to watch out for, my friend.

So, please just understand you don't need them.

Just because it's warm and fuzzy to hang out with them, they make us feel good, and they think like us, and they talk like us, it doesn't mean they're actually helping our business.

It's painful for me to say.

As a highly respected human being, I had to do that for myself.

I had to really dial back, like, "Man, am I really actually getting any value from these people?"

I even wondered what value even was, at one point.

Is it feeling good?

Is it social status?

Or, is it moving the needle in my business to make it serve me at the highest level possible?

Some of the people with the biggest and highest social statuses also have shit-show businesses.

I've seen that firsthand.

Despite what they portray to us, they don't actually make money.

Go look of the CEO's of some of the best-performing companies, they're not spending their time showing off their lifestyles or portraying this online image. They're not social influencers.

Why?

Because they're running their successful business. They don't need to do all that, it doesn't move the needle, at least not as much as going and doing the thing.

Unfortunately, most people are fighting not to help you to get results, but for your attention and then milking you like a goat.

They'll milk you like a goat right up until the point where you do not give them money anymore or your milk dries up, your bank account dries up. Then, they're gone.

I am not that.

Sticking with the goat example, I am of the mentality that I will continue to feed and water and I'll give you what you actually need because then you're going to produce more milk for me.

I don't want to just distract you and keep you here so I can milk you, milk you, milk you and then let you go when you're done. No.

I will give you what you need so you make more money, you can see all this is real, and then you'll give me more of it back, and you'll keep the difference.

Everyone wins that way.

That's the game, let's play it together and beat those fake gurus.

Remember, five bricks on that wall. We're on the same team.

Like I said before, with me, plan on having a fulfillment problem.

Plan on it.

It's not going to be that awesome at the time.

Counting the money will be, though, won't it?

Just remember this, Value Ladder and Dream 100™ is the secret sauce of all the big companies that have been around forever. All of them. And you're finally going to become a real company, soon, just like them.

Growing pains, though, those are a real thing.

Very real thing.

Growing pains are NOT getting ripped off by people stealing your money, clients abusing you, or pressure from bills every month.

No, growing pains are more like this. "Oh crap, we have too many customers and not enough ability to service them. We need to hire more people", or, "Uh oh, I need to raise my prices again because the demand for my service is too high", or, "Dang it, we ran out of books again because so many people want them", or, "Oops, we broke the Google Drive file because too many people are trying to download it".

Those are the problems I've had to deal with, and will be the type you'll have to deal with as you continue to implement what I tell you.

Then, your problems will become, "Oh no, we have a hundred thousand dollars in the bank account and that's about to all get taxed if we don't do something intelligent with it".

It's that kind of stuff that you have to figure out as you go.

Don't worry, they're all great problems, but they are problems.

Quick story.

A lot of times people don't talk enough about the before, they just want to talk about the after.

For a long time, my business was very up and down.

I was a full-time business owner throughout college and struggled for years.

There would be weeks when I would make no money at all and I'd get hit with this overwhelming feeling and pressure, "Oh my gosh, I have to make money."

I would just sit there and stop. I would sit in silence with myself. Almost like an intervention or sorts...

I'd say to myself, "Dana, what is happening, you have to make money, what are you doing?"

Then I would go do a bunch of crap and make money.

It was constant.

Up, down.

Up, then back down.

Maybe you're feeling a little bit of that right now where it's like, "Gosh, I just need to make more money"...

It's okay, help is on the way.

One of the worst things I've ever seen is people getting trapped in the illusion of progress...

Imagine this; spouses, families, marriages break up because of that, because this is the illusion, the person goes and starts consuming all this content from someone and the content never actually gives them the tangible result that they were promised in the first place.

They're left with an illusion of progress.

I've heard so many people say, "Oh, I listened to this podcast," or, "oh, watched this module of the course," or, "oh, I built this funnel," or, "oh, I started writing this book."

None of that is progress.

NONE of it.

"Oh, I designed this logo." That's not progress.

That's a STEP.

Here's where it's sad.

The spouse, let's say the husband for example, they got a full-time job and family...and are spending every waking hour outside of their job...working on their side business.

"Working" is actually consuming endless amounts of content that leads nowhere, and that gives no tangible tools.

Endless amounts.

They think they're getting somewhere.

You know where they're getting?

They're getting farther away from what matters, they're getting further away from their wife and their kids and even their job.

If that's not terrible enough...they're getting further away from themselves.

Inevitably, they end up losing everything...

I've had people literally tell me before, "Dana, I've listened to all these podcasts, followed these courses, and consumed so much stuff....but I still haven't made hardly any money".

To that, I say...

You ever see those Nigerian Princes that scam people and catfish them?

The victim gets incredibly invested, spending as much time and money as they can.

They're so far in, they literally can't believe that it's true, even when it's glaring them in the face. You'll see Dr. Phil, watch some of those clips. Dr. Phil will literally show these people that have been conned by this Nigerian Prince (to the tune of tens or even hundreds of thousands of dollars sometimes), and see indisputable proof that this person's not real.

Guess what happens...

They STILL somehow convince themselves that that's not real. That they weren't taken advantage of.

I'll wrap this up.

The husband is working so much on this side business that's getting nowhere because he never got any actual tools to use, never got any actual coaching or support to know what to do next, and then no accountability to make sure they did it.

They don't end up launching anything.

...and here's what they have to show for it: a LOT less money, a LOT less time spent with their spouse and kids, and still no progress.

You know what they should have done instead?

They should have shut all that off and they should have just spent that same amount of time with their kids and their wife, and they would have had more money and actually had something to show for it instead of being an ultimate failure.

That's the saddest part.

I hate that people do that to people.

It's not right.

That's why I wrote this, why you're reading it, and why that will change very soon.

Do all this stuff I'm saying and follow my lead, let me be one of the five in your world.

Please shut that other stuff off.

I know that you're probably feeling a little funky about, "I don't know, I don't think they'd do that to me."

Yeah, they are.

How am I so sure?

They did it to me, too.

Results don't lie.

In all that time you spent consuming that persons stuff and even feeling like you were making progress, how much ACTUAL progress did you make?

How much money did you make directly from them?

Any?

Have you made as much as you thought you would?

God forbid you've made more than what you've spent on it.

I understand, I get it. It took me $250,000 to discover this.

I would have rather spent that at the casino betting on black and saved all that time and stress.

You know what I mean? Just gotten it over with.

Double-down, let me be one of the five, please and thank you.

I'll give you my promise to you that I'll give you actual progress, and you'll see very soon...

We're almost there.

Keep reading, let's take this thing home.

Chapter #14

"Why Letting The Animal Out Of It's Cage Is The Best Thing That'll Happen To Your Business (You're Long Overdue!)"

I t's almost showtime! I get tagged all the time with folks saying they feel absolutely on fire with clarity and vision for what the heck it is they should be doing.

Let that sink in for a second.

Here's the crazy part.

With that clarity and re-igniting the fire within you...your relationships are going to benefit and personally, you're going to become a new person.

Now that might not happen today, but it's going to happen.

The more you get into my world, the more REVIVED you'll feel. It may sound a little out there, but it's true.

I feel it, myself.

My students and members feel it.

We feel alive.

We feel woken up.

That's what we do.

You will too, soon.

Like Galen.

Like Trent.

Like everyone.

You're going to find yourself back doing the things you love.

You'll be shutting off the stuff that you know is bad for you.

You'll be turning up the stuff you know is good for you.

Best of all, you'll be in complete control of the dial.

Maybe for the first time.

It's going to feel pretty dang good, isn't it?

I remember being back in college when I was first making a lot of money and doing well.

I remember I was doing all these cool things that I really was so proud of. Every Friday, I would go donate money to the food pantry.

At least once a week, I'd find somebody to buy their gas.

I would volunteer at church every Wednesday with the Youth Ministry.

I would do all these things because I felt so alive, and I felt so good. My business was doing great. For the first time in my life, I had a ton of money. I wanted to pay it forward.

I felt so free and awesome.

I remember I would go to the gym in the middle of the day, and I would think, "Man, it's nothing but me and a bunch of really old retired folks. This is so awesome. It's 11:00 a.m on a Tuesday, and I'm at the gym!"

Inevitably, things can't stay good forever.

Whether by your fault or not, all of a sudden, pressure is on again.

BAM!

You're right back into the battle and the grind.

It's like, dang, where did all my money go?

Then, your rent or mortgage comes due.

April 15 hits.

You have huge refund you need to give a client because they went crazy.

I wasn't good at managing a lot of money.

Too many times, I was right back in it.

For a while, I drifted into becoming lost.

I still was doing, comparatively, pretty well. But, I knew I had more that I should have been doing.

Ever feel that way?

It's really hard to go down to the food pantry and donate money when you don't have much.

I stopped doing that, and I was so disappointed in myself.

A few years went by where I simply lost focus.

Here's the good news.

I got back in, because of what I've laid out to you in this book, plus the tools and resources you're going to get into next.

You might also be wondering, "Dana, you made so much money in the Amazon game. Why did you get out of it?"

Fair question...

The truth: because this is more important.

Sure, I can go help somebody sell a lot more Garcinia Cambogia on Amazon, yeah.

But, is that really changing the world though? Is that really impacting people the way that I know I can? No.

Brutal honesty.

That's why I'm writing this all these years later.

It's not because I'm going to get rich from this book.

It's math, I can't get rich off of it.

It's because I'm able to help you and impact you.

Quick story.

I bought an office building a few years ago, which was one of the biggest tangible purchases I've ever made in my business (outside of the cumulated over the last decade wasted money on people that sucked, of course).

I bought a relatively large, 2,500 square foot office and completely renovated it.

The main reason was to house my Pet Supplements company which, at the time, had eight employees.

It was really cranking, and I ended up selling that business. With that, I had to let everybody go. It was tough. It was very tough.

Remember, the business doesn't have feelings and doesn't care. But, I do.

I just sat by myself in that office, 2,500 square foot, by myself. I'm like, "Oh man, this is lonely. This is way more lonely than it was before."

Little by little, day by day I just started visualizing something...

Then finally, it hit me!

"Wow, I have all this space right here that I'm not using (where we used to produce the supplements)...why don't I make that a classroom? Why don't I have people come here, in person?", I thought to myself.

So I did, I completely renovated the entire office to host people.

Now, I'm very happy. I've got what I would consider a world-class office to host masterminds and retreats, which I do every month.

I bring folks from all ends of the world to the sleepy little town of Clear Lake, Wisconsin.

I hope to meet you at one of my events, soon.

I'll leave you with the story of Carlotta, a gal who came to one of our retreats. It was a two-day book-writing retreat where you come with wherever your book is...and leave with it 80-95% DONE.

It's a pretty cool, intense thing.

Carlotta hopped in an airplane and came to Wisconsin from Arkansas.

She's is a former IRS agent who now helps entrepreneurs. She's sitting on the other side of the table during the audit, which is really fascinating.

She showed up, and like most, didn't quite know what to expect. Very kind, smart gal.

I think it's one of those things where it never seems to fail. Every time you go somewhere for something, even like you reading this book, you go for one thing...but end up leaving with something else.

Usually, that something else that you leave with is WAY better.

For example.

You go to an event.

You think there's going to be an awesome nugget of value and wisdom. You don't get it, but then you met someone amazing, and that someone amazing led you to something incredible...like a partnership or connection that you would have never been able to pull on your own.

That's way better, anyway.

Happened for Carlotta, too.

She came to get her book done, which she did.

BUT...she left with clarity, permission and a clear plan to ramp her business and spread her mission...which is the thing she knew she needed to be doing for years.

She just didn't quite know how.

She trusted the process, came up to the retreat and allowed my team and me to help get that out (just like we do with countless people, every day).

I won't forget that moment, at the end of the retreat...her telling us how the book was awesome and all, but the permission and clarity she was leaving with was absolutely priceless.

We were all in tears.

It's so fun to watch her owning that, to this day. She is on fire with clarity and vision, just like what I said.

I know her relationships are benefiting. All of her team members, I can tell the dynamic has shifted. It's almost like the pendulum has swung back in her favor.

Now, it's your turn.

If you've got a level of frustration somewhere, it's going to go away.

Whatever you've been waiting to do.

Whatever you've been holding back from.

It's all going to change.

I'm telling you.

You follow my lead, you enter my world, you're not going to want to get out. (Sorry in advance)

That's because this is a long time coming.

Keep reading, we're almost there.

It's almost your time to take back control, and get the pendulum swinging back...and play the game the RIGHT way.

Chapter #15
"A Quick Look Into The Future."

I don't know about you, but I can't keep a secret for the life of me. When I bought my wife's engagement ring, it was like the roughest two months of my life.

I hid it in a spot where I thought she'd NEVER see it.

On the way upper shelf of the closet of our guest bedroom. I don't think she'd ever been in there, to that point.

Of course, about a week out from the big day that I planned to pop the question...there she was. Standing on a chair, reaching for something on the top shelf of the closet...right next to where the ring was hidden.

In an absolute panic, the only thing I could think to do...was yell, "Run!"

She looked at me, confused, and asked, "Why?"...

Instinctually, still in a panic, I replied, "My stomach hurts really bad and it's about to smell terrible in here...".

By gosh, it worked.

She may not have ran to evacuate, but it was exactly what I needed to direct her attention away from that shelf...and bought me enough time to sneak up there and relocated the ring.

With that, I'm going to give you a few spoilers...

There's SO MUCH more beyond what I've laid out in this book.

This is a fantastic foundation, to which you're now going to be able to play the game...instead of get played...

...now, it's time to WIN!

Let's start thinking Dream 100™, since that's the next step and, ultimately, is how to win.

Think about who you already have existing in your network that you could possibly go and plug into the missing spots on your Value Ladder.

Sometimes, we have the answer inside of us...we just need to find it.

That's the lowest hanging fruit, and I'll walk you through that too, inside the Dream 100™ Book & Challenge.

I did this, myself, by the way.

A few years back, I did a webinar that went crazy. $206,304 in 90 minutes.

At the time, that was nearly as much money as I'd made the entire year prior.

Want to know how that happened?

Well, it started with running two webinars before that...that absolutely tanked.

Both of those only had one thing in common, I tried Facebook ads for the traffic.

I was like, "Oh boy, this doesn't work".

Then, too stubborn to quit, I did exactly what I just told you to do and I tapped into the Dream 100™, going after my existing network.

I happened to have a guy named James who has a software that paired perfectly with my offer, plus a large audience that would want and need it.

I called him up and I said, "Hey man, I've got this killer webinar, it's been converting like crazy," (wink wink, right).

Seriously though, I was like, "You ready to promote this to your audience?"

And he said, "Yes, sure."

I said to myself, "What? You said yes?"

So we did it, and low and behold, the same exact webinar, didn't tank.

$206,304 in sales.

I was like, "Yep, the Dream 100™ works."

So, tap into your existing network, that's number one.

Number two, don't think you need to limit the people that you're plugging into those spots to one person.

In fact, I would advise against that.

The Dream 100™ done correctly is all about diversity and sustainability.

So, if, for example, you plug someone into one of the spots and you refer people to them and you get a commission or vice versa and they get hit by a bus or something happens that's bad, you don't want to have to go find another person.

Always have a backup.

It's always better to have more than enough.

The third thing I would highly recommend is when you are Dream 100™'ing, do this.

One of the biggest questions that I run into when people are setting all this up is, "How does commission work, what do I do to incentivize them to prescribe me?"

You'll get a deep-dive inside the Dream 100™ Challenge, but one of the big things is making sure that you understand that they're motivated by two things...and only two things...

1) Even more important than money, is if your thing makes their thing better.

Read that again.

If your thing enhances the result of their thing, they're pretty much forced to prescribe it.

Like, for example, James.

My Amazon books (what we were offering on the webinar) made his software more effective and made his software users, cause they're amazon sellers, made them more money...which in turn made them stick on his software longer or be able to afford more features.

All of that also had the ripple effect of making James look like a hero because he was helping all of his customers, by prescribing me.

THAT is what will blow your business up, and will cause you to have folks banging on your door to prescribe your products or services to their audiences.

This is a very simplified way of looking at it, but it's true.

I'll of course get into the weeds of it and show you how plus give you to the tools you need inside the Challenge, but you'll get there.

2) The second thing that they're motivated by is money.

They're not going to operate like a charity, unless they're a charity.

They need money.

Here's what they're doing...

They're weighing their time of basically creating the thing that you've created versus just letting you do it because you've already created it.

Like, James could have thought, "I've got 50% commission coming on this offer. It sounds like a great offer and something my audience wants. Should I create it, or hire someone to create it and sell it on my own, to keep 100%? Or, just take the faster/easier route and prescribe Dana's offer?"

James chose wisely 😊

Remember the whole, "What's gotten you here will get you there as long as you innovate it", I talked about earlier?

James thought, "Ah that's not really what I do, I'm a software guy, so I should just take 50%. A lot easier and faster and let him be the expert, right."

It's got to make sense for them to do it or else they won't.

These are just a few quick tactics to think about implementing right as you get ready to deploy your Dream 100™ campaigns...

That gets the engine started, but to get the wheels turning, again, Dream 100™ Book and Challenge have all the good stuff.

A quick story that really illustrate these tactics in action.

Let's talk about Shane.

Shane joined my world a few months back, and I don't even think he knew why.

He just knew he had some problems he needed to solve.

To that point, he never made a dime online...so he went ahead and joined.

He did exactly what I'm telling you to do: bought my books, joined my challenges, immersed himself in it and did everything that I told him to.

He owns a restoration company, by trade.

They're the guys that go in and clean up and restore a basement when it gets flooded, or a garage if it's been in a fire.

He owns a thriving offline brick and mortar local business out of Tennessee.

Now, he's launched a program that helps other restoration contractors, like himself, to improve their sales and marketing (cause that's something he's really good at).

He wanted to take his thing mainstream and kind of maxed out what he was doing locally, so he created that program and he followed my lead.

He's got his Value Ladder perfectly laid out...plus has deployed the Dream 100™ perfectly.

Now, instead of spinning his wheels, wondering if this whole "online thing" would ever work for him...

...he keeps tagging me all the time, going crazy about how he's making more money now passively from his restoration coaching and consulting business than he is through his actual restoration business!

So cool.

Although Shane's results aren't typical, neither is he.

Real quick, let me share about Renee. This story is crazy.

Renee is one of the folks that invested in my Dream 100™ Book back when it was originally $2,000.

Full disclosure: she initially thought she got scammed.

Frankly, I don't blame her because I guess logically you would think it would come with a bunch more stuff...but it didn't...it was just the book.

Remember, though, that's how valuable it is, it's worth $2,000 on its own.

She was sick to her stomach after she bought it.

I remember her telling me that she kept that investment private from her husband.

A few weeks after the book showed up, she sent me a video message explaining how she thought she'd just been scammed...to then actually reading it.

She implemented everything she discovered inside, and went from struggling to make $10,000 in a month all the way up to, now she's doing six-figure launches when she wants and it's really cool and it's all because of Value Ladder + Dream 100™.

And by the way these results are not typical, obviously. But neither is Renee.

But then one of my favorites is with one of my Dream 100™ Mastermind members, Christian.

He came into my world, same reason.

Had some problems in his business, wanted to make more money, wasn't really sure, knew that I seem at least a genuine human being and was drawn by that.

Christian's a Grammy-nominated music artist, super talented.

He's got a business where he creates custom songs for people.

After working with me for a while, going through my stuff he created, he's got two lanes that he runs now.

He has more clarity about what the heck he's doing than ever before.

In one lane, he creates custom love songs for weddings and anniversary presents.

In the other lane, he creates legacy songs for folks that have passed away to solidify their memory.

Christian did exactly what I told him to…

His Value Ladder is DIALED-IN…and now has people in his Dream 100™ List that prescribe him free clients to his large packaged.

He's getting leads that turn into thousands, if not tens of thousands of dollars, per client.

It's all thanks to all the time, trust, and effort he put in.

Christian's awesome and although his results aren't typical, he's the man.

I actually had him come out and perform a custom love song at my wedding, live.

Last person I'll mention is Ross.

Ross is crazy smart.

He's also an old-school, no-nonsense, shoot-me-straight, give me the good stuff kind of guy.

He read through my books, inhaled them.

He said, "Oh, that's the stuff. I just want all of it", and started throwing money at my programs.

He joined the award-winning Dream 100™ Launch Program.

On day two, I believe he still has the record, of joining...not even 10% through the program and the membership area...he landed a deal that got him an R.O.I.

Actually, MORE than an R.O.I. on the program.

He landed a deal with one of this Dream 100™ Targets worth $25,000/more...on day 2!

Ross definitely isn't a normal guy, and his results aren't typical, but DANG!

I can't take all this credit, of course.

It's a matter of surrounding yourself with the right five bricks, isn't it?

When you do that, you unlock some pretty cool stuff.

I know, I know.

You've tried things in the past that failed.

Social media marketing.

Facebook ads.

Marketing "experts".

Other books or courses.

Other coaching programs.

I get it.

Remember...I tried them, too.

The real reason they didn't work I've already outlined.

Now you know.

People aren't out for results, they're out for the illusion of results just to keep your attention...which keeps your wallet close.

It's no longer the information age we're in, information has become so saturated that we are now in the attention age.

Their goal is just to keep your attention, that's it.

They don't care about your results.

Screw results, results are hard.

They just want your attention and to get you to FEEL like you're getting results.

That's easy.

And it's very sad, so I hope that makes you understand and appreciate why that stuff didn't work...which became a $250,000 lesson for me.

No mistakes, just lessons.

Don't forget about the "no-no's", especially trying to do this on your own.

Remember, I've put over twelve years into this and I've worked with literally thousands of entrepreneurs one-on-one to be able to get this message across to you.

And I'll leave you with this, if you do nothing else but just trust in the fact that I am a person that uses the stuff I tell you to do and sell to you...you'll be fine.

Let common sense be your new ruler.

If the funnel builder was so good at building million-dollar funnels, he would build his own million-dollar funnels.

If the Facebook ads expert was so good at running Facebook ad traffic, they would run their own traffic.

If the coach was so good at coaching, he would coach himself.

Right?

They're out there selling things that they don't actually do, and now you know better.

The next time you consider Dream 100™'ing someone, hiring someone, buying something else, or even just listening or watching something...remember those very powerful two words: Prove it.

...I'll drink my own Kool-Aid one last time, and Prove it.

If you haven't, yet, head over to --> www.IsDanaLegit.com

Let it load, it's going to be a minute.

There are probably more than a thousand stories on that page from people that I have worked with, personally.

I didn't prompt and I didn't beg or ask.

They just send them to me.

I hope to see your story on there, too.

I proved it through this book.

Now, I want you to prove it by inhaling the Dream 100™ Book, and then the Dream 100™ Challenge.

Go all-in and immerse yourself.

You have my complete and utter heartfelt sincere word that I will not disappoint you and I will not let you down, if you follow my lead.

I am the breath of fresh air in this crazy world we live in.

That's my promise to you.

We'll see you inside my Dream 100™ Value Ladder...as you'll climb that at your own pace.

What's sure is this: I'll see you at the top!

Welcome to the family.

Your Next Steps...

(DON'T MISS THIS)

STEP #1, Complete Your Value Ladder:

I've already done all the heavy lifting, just fill out a quick form (100% FREE!) and watch your Value Ladder come together perfectly! Go ahead and finish up your Value Ladder the RIGHT way with the FREE Value Ladder Challenge I put together for you, so you can make sure you're doing it absolutely perfectly and your business is set on the path for success!

>> www.ValueLadderChallenge.com

STEP #2, Inhale Dream 100™ Book:

Having your Value Ladder built out is the first half of the success equation, now finish the second half! Grab a copy of my award-winning Dream 100™ Book to get clear on exactly how you should be Dream 100™'ing the RIGHT way! (Same exact book I used to charge $2,000 for...you get a copy for FREE, just pay for S&H) Page 29 has something naughty, hope that's okay! 😉

>> www.Dream100Book.com/free

STEP #3, Join Dream 100™ Challenge:

Don't recreate the wheel! I've got all the tools you need to figure out WHO your Dream 100™ is...WHERE to find them...and WHAT to say to them! Don't do this wrong! "Spam 100'ing" is NOT going to work...and you don't want to have to figure all this out on your own, join the Dream 100™ and leverage the tools I already created! It's super easy to get through (no nonsense or wasted fluff), and very affordable! Join now!

>> www.Dream100Challenge.com

STEP #4, Unlock Dream 100™ Book: Reloaded!:

There's a SEQUEL to the Dream 100™ Book...and it's PACKED with value! The sequel, called the Dream 100™ Book: Reloaded! is absolutely jam-packed with never-before-seen Dream 100™ GOLD! It's actually the LARGEST marketing book in history, coming in at a staggering 1,055 pages! No, it's never going to be available for sale...the ONLY way to get a copy is to complete the Dream 100™ Challenge! (We'll rush-ship you a copy for FREE after completing!)

>> www.ClaimReloaded.com

STEP #5, Apply For Award-Winning Dream 100™ Launch Program:

Ready to take your Dream 100™'ing to the max?! Apply to join the very private, award-winning Dream 100™ Launch Program that includes private weekly group coaching...additional tools and resources you'll NEVER find anywhere else...closed-door meetings...and more! By the second day in, you'll know this was the right decision.

>> www.Dream100Launch.com/join

There is N.O.T.H.I.N.G. else like this. Please do not miss your shot at getting in this program.

See you inside!

I need a favor...Can you share your thoughts on my book? I'd love to hear from you! Simply email me:
(info@derricksgroup.com)

PS! You did it. I'm so proud, you've just been awoken...enlightened...and empowered to take back control of your business and play the game to WIN. Remember, this isn't the end...it's the beginning. Keep going and follow my lead.

Printed in Great Britain
by Amazon